Live LIVE!

Live LIVE!

KATIE O'CONNELL

NEW DEGREE PRESS

Live LIVE!

ISBN   978-1-64137-228-2   *Paperback*

         978-1-64137-229-9   *Ebook*

This book is dedicated to _____.
name

Everyone has a story worth telling. May this book inspire

_____ *to live LIVE in the present,*
name
taking control of your story.

ACKNOWLEDGMENTS

———

A special thank you to the Edward M. Muldoon Center for Entrepreneurship at John Carroll University, and especially Dr. Doan Winkel, for supporting and empowering me to be the author of my own story.

I would also like to thank:

My parents, Mike and Kara, for setting the foundation to my story and inspiring me to live a life of service and community building.

The interviewees whose names you will read on the pages of this book and those whose voice influenced the arch of the story. Your experience and passion illustrate a vibrant life of purpose and adventure.

The Team at New Degree Press for leading me through this creative journey. The team includes Eric Koster, Brian Bies, Carson Schutter, NeKisha Wilkins, Ryan Porter, Dania Zafar, and Mateusz Cichosz.

The 33 backers whose financial support allowed me to transform countless pages of notes and interviews into the book you are about to read.

The number of friends who doubled as cheerleaders and collaborators in the ideation, research, pre-reader, and launch phase of my book.

CONTENTS

Live LIVE!

Live /liv/

1. to remain alive
2. make one's home in a particular place or with a particular person.

LIVE! /līv/

1. not dead or inanimate; living.
2. relating to a musical performance given in concert, not on a recording.

Live LIVE! /liv līv/

1. to remain present in the vibrancy of the given experience
2. not aimless; on a purposeful adventure

Live LIVE! SOUNDTRACK

———

Many songs influenced the making of this book.

Some of the songs you will find sprinkled in the pages, part of the story of those I interviewed. Others songs rang through my ears during the long hours of writing and kept me sane through the process. These songs are the soundtrack to *Live LIVE!*

Enjoy on Spotify as you read along: https://spoti.fi/2F8mGtc

INTRODUCTION

———

I didn't go to Woodstock.

My knowledge of Woodstock is best summarized by comedian Demetri Martin:

"I know about Woodstock probably as much as your average person who is over 30, where I'd know Jimi Hendrix, Janis Joplin, Grateful Dead."[1]

But hearing the way people who did attend Woodstock talk about it makes me wish I had. Woodstock was a unique connection between the most talented musicians in the world, a world at war and full of strife, and an audience that was high on life and on a few other things. It's a cultural phenomenon that was so perfect you couldn't— and the organizers didn't— plan it to be that way.

What does my generation have?

Fyre Festival.

* *

At the tail end of the millennial generation, I, like many other millennials, became obsessed with creating, sharing, and capturing memories. According to a study conducted by Eventbrite, three in four millennials are spending their money on experiences rather than things. Millennials command an estimated $1.3 trillion in annual consumer spending and are dedicating more of their income to experiences in hopes they won't catch a case of FOMO (fear of missing out). For 69% of millennials, they leave events feeling more connected to other people, the community, and the world.[2] They are bonding with loved ones at these experiences, tweeting and posting on social media for the rest of the world to see. Through these events they are creating their identity, an identity that is becoming ever more essential as technology dominates the job market.

And yet if we look at the way we currently experience live events — and more specifically live music — it's less Woodstock and more Frye.

We want to experience amazing, unique, life-changing live events so that we can post about them on social media.

I wonder what Woodstock would have been like in the era of Snapchat and Instagram? What would we learn about the human experience? Or human connection?

Chinese business magnate Jack Ma is the co-founder and executive of Alibaba Group, a multinational technology conglomerate and one of the largest profiting companies in the world. At the World Economic Forum in 2018 he argued against artificial intelligence education and supported art-based education.

Seems counterintuitive coming from a guy who built his wealth on technology, but he says, "If we do not change the way we teach, 30 years from now we'll be in trouble. The things we teach our children are things from the past 200 years – it's knowledge-based. And we cannot teach our kids to compete with machines, they are smarter." [3]

No machine can process the values and skills of a human being, from independent thinking to teamwork. Art-based education provides kids with a foundation in creative problem-solving, collaboration, resourcefulness, leadership, resilience, and empathy.

Ma suggests, "We should teach our kids sports, music, painting – the arts – to make sure that they are different. Everything we teach should make them different from machines." [4]

Humans need to be humans, not machines. How do we do that? It's through art, sports, music and events.

- Art, as a vehicle of expression, will always need the human touch.
- Sports, as an activity for physical exertion, need physical humans' effort.
- Music, as vocal or instrumental performance, needs human lungs, hands, and hearts to be performed.
- Events, as curated human experiences and entertainment, need the human touch.

Human passion will soon outweigh human knowledge— machines will outsmart us there.

Getting back to what makes something human, I ask, would it be possible to recreate what was special about Woodstock today? In August of 2017, I had an experience that convinced me we could.

My friend Caitlin called me over the summer and said, "You have to go to a Sofar Sounds show."

A few weeks later we found ourselves on the rooftop of a docked boat overlooking the Cleveland skyline. The sun hung low and the air smelled like the end of summer as we laid our blanket just feet from the string of Christmas lights enclosing what would be the main stage that night. People poured in, some with blankets, others with guitars; it was hard to tell who was going to perform and who was there to listen. As the sun began to set, a women with deep maroon lipstick and long dark hair grabbed the mic and said, "Welcome to Sofar! Are you all excited?" The crowd chattered back, adding to the good vibes.

"My name is Jeanette and I am the Director of Sofar Sounds here in Cleveland. Who has been to a Sofar show before?" About a third of the crowd raised their hands, answering Jeanette's question. People yelled out that they had been to shows in Detroit, London, and Toronto, just a few of the 400+ cities Sofar now does shows in.

As the sky melted into shades of pinks and oranges, four artists took center stage for a twenty-minute set. In between acts we were prompted by Jeanette to make friends with the listeners around us.

I left elated, as if I had lifted this heavyweight pressing on my chest that had become such a normalcy, I had hardly realized it was there. Music was an integral part of my daily life, I sang in the choir and wrote music with a friend. In the past few years, I had parted from music in this intimate way and attempted to fill that void going to local venues to see touring bands a couple of times a month. That night was different. I felt as though I had just uncovered a hidden gem in live music. It brought me back in an intimate experience with music and to the people around me. I wasn't sure if I wanted to shout and tell the world, or keep it close to my heart and save the experiences for myself.

I wondered, where else these music experiences were hiding? How would we recreate the music experience if we started from scratch? Will we ever find our own Woodstock?

That night at Sofar, I found a piece of my Woodstock. I felt a sense of belonging for the first time in a long time. While it took me a while to admit it, I wrote this book as a journey of self exploration, looking for a recipe for belonging in my own life:

- A recipe for a community in which I could feel completely and utterly my most authentic self.
- A way of rewriting music back into my life, recognizing that music fulfills me and allows me to feel alive. I lost track of my relationship with music over the past four years and this is my proclamation that music is again part of my life.

- A means of discovering my own Woodstock — and one that we all can develop for ourselves.

My passion lies in creating community, human-centric experiences, and creating a sense of belonging for others by aligning the talents of different people to put an event together that is transformational. Each individual has a unique talent, skillset, passion, and ideas. When given the proper platform to share that, amazing things take place. Our world has an unbelievable amount of resources offered by each individual and we just need to figure out the right way to connect them all so we as a community can unlock our full potential.

That is as true in the music scene as in any other industry. I believe my purpose in this work is to be a connector, telling people's stories, seeing where talents, skill sets, and passions overlap and bringing them together.

And so if I was going to redesign an in-person, musical experience from the ground up, I'd need to forget everything and start fresh.

I began talking with community builders from across the country on how they create engaging, meaningful experiences. In the process, I found myself most excited to talk with people in the music scene. I talked to people at Sofar, a global movement of intimate shows, and at Superfly, a company putting on some of the biggest US music festivals, and everything in between.

* *

Along the way I realized the best live music event did not take place on a farm in 1968 in upstate New York, and it's nothing like Fyre festival; it's yet to be created.

I realized something powerful:

- **This book isn't to help you find <u>the next</u> Woodstock experience.**
- **This book is to help you create <u>your next</u> Woodstock experience.**

You see, I discovered that each of us can create our own "best music experience" in our hometown, in our local clubs, with our favorite music, and with a group of strangers or a group of friends.

Today no one will create the experience for us; we will have to find our own, and this book captures dozens of stories, teachings, lessons and insights that you can leverage to discover what will help you create your perfect live experience.

Turns out, LIVE is the only way to live!

HOW TO USE THIS BOOK

———

Treat this book like a buffet. Made up of a number of short stories, each chapter provides ingredients to the ultimate live music recipe. These ingredients also have hints within, a sort of tasting guide, that will help you savor all the flavor live music offers.

Before you start this book, ask yourself, what is missing from your current live music experience?

Pass on what is not appetizing to you.

This book is broken up into three sections:

- LIVE Music from Within – ingredients from unique, out of the box, live music experiences.

- LIVE Music from Beyond – ingredients from community events that offer lessons for the live music space.
- LIVE Music: Recipe & Tasting Guide – where we get cooking and put it all together.

This book is meant to be fun to read. Treat every chapter as its own snack and only take the time for those that appeal to you. Each chapter is marked as a tool for our chefs and hungry patrons. Who are you?

The chef = promoter, venue owner, concert host, artist, band, or event organizers

Hungry patron = fans or concert-goers.

To our hungry patrons, do you ever appreciate something more when you know the backstory? Maybe you like your local barber because they are a friend or shop at a particular store because they support a social cause you care about. We invite you to read what our Chefs are up to; we think it will help you appreciate the live music experience that much more.

Do you not fall into the chef or hungry patron category?

Music is the case study for how to create community in any live event or experience. There are lessons embedded in each page for community creators to bring more purpose and intention to events they host. There are nuggets of wisdom from the many insightful people I talked to in this process that invite us to open our eyes to the possibilities around us each day. This book is designed to help you think outside the box and craft the perfect meal for yourself in live music and in any avenue of your life.

Take a seat at the table and enjoy!

With a new set of ingredients in front of you and some old favorites I pulled out that were hiding in the back of the pantry, it's time to get cooking! Part three of this book offers the chefs a recipe for live music experiences and a tasting guide for the hungry patrons.

The best recipes are the ones that are shared.

The best way to build community is by breaking bread.

So as you finish this book share it at the table, enjoy, and live LIVE!

PART 1

LIVE MUSIC: INGREDIENTS FROM WITHIN

In dive bars, concert halls, and on festival grounds the vibrations of feet stomping intertwine with waves of melodic soprano voices and rhythmic drum banging. These are places where music lives and music belongs. Where people know they can come in search for a musical escape and partake in an energy release through sound and movement.

In this section, you will read stories from friends who were front and center in some of the most authentic, raw, live music experiences. Through the stories of friends I made in my journey writing this book, you will experience a festival on a cruise oasis in the Atlantic Ocean, a part block party, part dance hall brunch in Los Angeles, a concert in the rock and roll capital, and a collaborative album in the making on a road trip across the United States. Watch as strangers become friends and bands tear down walls, befriending fans.

Each live music experience offers something special, an ingredient to creating a community-based experience around live music. Music has brought people together for tens of thousands of years. No event brings us closer together quite like live music. From creating a space to developing a presence, these ingredients offer unique elements that bring vibrant life into the live experience.

In the digital age sacred music spaces have been invaded by cameras hungry for Snapchat and Instagram content. They have become exclusive events thanks to penny pinching scalpers. In the heat of the music industry standards, they have become a mere production rather than a true art form. They are a place for socializing, a bar first and a listening room second.

That is not to say that every venue has been overtaken by iPhone screens, scalpers' schemes, overproduction, and social butterflies, but it is important to remember that people tend to be more distracted than ever in the digital age. As a result, the way we experience music, art, sports, entertainment, work, school, and day-to-day life is changing. Now more than ever we feel a need to find belonging.

In the United States, 46% of the entire population regularly feels lonely in the most connected time in human history. [5] Loneliness is subjective, and even people with the best social skills can experience loneliness. Loneliness is a bodily function like hunger. Hunger makes you pay attention to your physical needs while loneliness makes you pay attention to your social needs. Loneliness is a craving for socialization. Music is highly acclaimed for its pleasurable powers for the individual but often overlooked for the impact it's impact on our social well being. Music connects circuits in the brain that create empathy, trust, cooperation, and satisfying our social cravings, curing loneliness.

In an article published in the Greater Good Magazine at the University of California, Berkeley, three scientists' anecdotes illustrate how music creates a sense of belonging, a social buzz, through shared experience. Here is what they found:

1. We stream music anytime, anywhere these days, but long before Spotify, iTunes, CDs, cassette tapes, records, and even phonautograms, the only way to listen to music was live. People came in contact with one another for performances. Together, our early ancestors were provided physical and psychological comfort through music. Today, we still survive and thrive because of live music that brings us together. Before a baseball game begins, fans sing the national anthem. In this moment, a sense

of safety, obligation, and belonging to the team, and the community that comes with it, is communicated.[6] There is something special in knowing that you are part of an age-old tradition that has stood the test of time.

2. A good concert might call for crowd participation – clapping, snapping, and singing along. When people coordinate sound and movement with those around them, the human brain experiences positive social feelings towards those they are in sync with.[7] When we are one unit, in sync with the people around us, endorphins release. Think about the flip side of things: have you gotten pissed off when the guy next to you is trailing behind, clapping off beat? Perhaps shot the screamer behind you a look? You had this negative reaction because they were getting in the way of your endorphins.

3. When people sing, they release oxytocin, dubbed the love hormone.[8] Scientists found that individuals, tone deaf singers and rockstars alike, who sang for thirty minutes a day had significantly more oxytocin in their bloodstream even if they were not experiencing joy in the moment of the act. Perhaps new mothers sing lullabies to babies to form a bond through oxytocin release.

Music influences how we interact with one another and with the world. Live music has proven to be a method of survival, providing us with a resource for our basic needs of safety, connection to a unit, and love.

We associate certain styles of music with certain values, personality types, and lifestyles. Just as we all have our own taste in music, I have my own. With close to 35,000 concerts and festivals in 2018 in the US promoted by Live Nation alone, there are a lot of choices.[9] This section of *Live LIVE!* skims the surface of what is happening here in the United States., primarily off the beaten path of stadium arenas and major music festivals. I didn't dive into the places you might expect when you think about community surrounding live music. I did not turn to the Grateful Dead or Burning Man even though there is a lot to learn from the communities that follow this band and festival. I took the road less traveled and now it's your turn to do the same.

Sit back, relax and Live LIVE!

CHAPTER 1

LIVE MUSIC IS A CITY IF YOU CALL IT WHAT YOU WANT

"Miss Jackson" by OutKast made Atlanta home to the hip-hop revolution. "My Girl" by the Temptations showed there was more than car manufacturing happening in Detroit. "California Love" by 2pac featuring Dr. Dre showed regional pride for the city of Compton.

Atlanta.

Detroit.

Compton.

It's not a stretch to call all of them "music towns." But why?

These cities were not orchestrating a movement to make these hits happen. They were not doing anything to claim their titles as "music cities"; they just did.

These cities were lucky to have a golden ticket— an uber talented artist— fall into their lap. "Miss Jackson," "My Girl," and "California Love" have become inseparable from their city's identities and put these places on the map as "music cities."

However, not every record label happens to open their doors in a Detroit neighborhood and have Mable John, Eddie Holland, and Mary Wells as neighbors, not to mention Michael Jackson, Diana Ross, and Stevie Wonders in the Motown Era in years to come. So can one design a music city, or do they just have to sit and hope they might catch lightning in a bottle?

There is no formula for catching lightning in a bottle.

When a city's people and leadership acknowledge music is a necessity, that is when a city becomes a music city. As Elizabeth Cawein puts it, "Music is about so much more than hits."[10]

As Cawein suggests, music is not about the top ten songs that are being pumped out of corporate high rises in New York City or along Music Row in Nashville. Music is a way to navigate life. It makes us smarter, healthier and happier. There is no need to wait for a smashing hit to put a city on the map. When a city whole-heartedly recognizes music as a necessity, then it can start calling itself a music city.

That's what Austin, Texas did.

In 1991, Austin took a step back and looked at its assets.

Cawein defines assets as the number of recording studios, record labels, historic landmarks, music clubs, free jazz nights, weekly folk jam sessions, music schools, instrument shops, and anything else that serves as a music platform and incubator.[11] Back in 1991, Austin had over 250 music venues to catch an indie, rock, country, or jazz show at sunrise to well beyond sunset. Boasting over 1,900 bands and more live music venues per capita than anywhere else in the world, Austin branded itself as the "Live Music Capital of the World" and owned it.

The first step is to determine the city's assets and the second is to get to know the challenges. Cawein takes a holistic approach, asking questions like:

- Are the venues struggling?
- Is there a venue ladder for artists to move up or are they expected to make the jump from coffee shop to coliseum?
- What does the city's infrastructure look like?
- Is there good public transportation?
- Is the cost of living affordable?
- How is gentrification affecting neighborhoods?[12]

Austin saw a musical momentum percolating and asked these difficult questions. By naming and owning their reputation as the "Live Music Capital of the World" new venues opened, existing spaces brought in live acts, and locals and tourists brought into the music-centric culture. Austin did not check off all the criteria for a "perfect music city" but instead focused on their assets and backed them with excitement and energy.

"When we look inward, we create that place that musicians want to live. And when we look outward, we build opportunities for them to advance their career while also driving attention back to our city and leveraging music as a talent-attraction tool,"[13] Cawein says. Cities must look inward to create a place musicians want to live before they look outward creating structure and defining what it is in it for them, as a city, in our capitalistic world.

Cawein proclaims the third step is about leadership and strategy.[14] Cities like Berlin, Paris, and yes, Austin, give musicians a seat at the table. Austin Music Commission advises the City Council on the development of the music industry. They are apart of the implementation process when new programs are created. Citizens can move the needle in their city by voting representatives into power that value musicians voices and see their product, music, as a necessity.

Any City is A Music City; Every City is a Music City

Any city that starts moving its feet to the beat, opening its ears to the harmonies echoing through the streets, and spending its dollars on concert tickets and bar cover charges will elevate its musically talented inhabitants. Any city that starts using its voice to celebrate its talent will empower the music scene.

Music became a necessity in Austin.

Its residents did not wait for their OutKast, Temptations, or 2pac to stroll through. They leaned in to their assets and developed their best qualities, maximizing to make the good great. As a result, a community emerged that locals proudly call their own and tourists make a priority on their bucket list.

> **Queue *Call It What You Want* by Foster the People**
>
> *We've got nothing to prove*
> *Your social guides give you swollen eyes*
> *But what I've got can't be bought so you can just*
> *Call it what you want*

Ingredients

Call it what you want and own it.

No waiting for lightning in a bottle. Know your assets, understand the hurdles, and create a strategy backed by leaders. That's how business works, a city is no different. A venue is no different. Wherever there is music, there must be an awareness of the assets, hurdles, and strategy.

Take Orange Bowl 2018 for example. Dave Matthews's band and Walk the Moon played at the Capitol One Beach Bash, a free concert on Miami Beach before kickoff.

The asset: a captive audience.
The hurdle: not being the main attraction.
The strategy: market as a two-for-one deal.

People left saying they didn't just go to the big game but they also boasted about the free show they got to see. Suddenly, Orange Bowl gained a reputation not only as the annual American college football bowl game but also as a multidimensional entertainment experience.

CHAPTER 2

LIVE MUSIC IS ON THE STREET IF YOU LISTEN

———

"A warm can of beer for your troubles" was the payment Ryan O'Reilly was getting for five act bills as a singer songwriter in London bars during his time in university.

The mentality in these London venues was, and many cases still is, musicians "pay to play." Artist sell tickets and bring fans to the venue, not the other way around. It is a horrible trap that many young artists like Ryan fall into.

The first show was amazing. All of Ryan's friends came and they were excited to be there for his big debut. Yet, for every gig to follow the crowd cut in half, dwindling in size until it was the one-hundredth show and Ryan found himself dragging three friends along to see him play the same tunes.

Raised in Southampton, England, his Irish parentage and English upbringing led to him being a great storyteller. When he graduated from university, he lived with a group of friends, his band, in South London. They started street performing to pay some of the bills, following the lead of the street performers in their neighborhood. Floating around London, the crew played originals. Ryan joked, "I'm too stupid to play covers, can't remember other people's words and learn the proper way."

The crew rolled out of bed to play hungover in the streets again and again. With time, the mentality shifted. They started to show up a little earlier and appear more presentable. "I didn't want to be a busker," Ryan said. "We were a band that happened to be performing on the street."

To claim their status as a band of street performers rather than buskers and prove they were worth more than spare change, they needed something that they could sell. So, they recorded a live album in a bar with friends from university. Over four years, 5,000 people would pick up that album, a time capsule of the band's story. Their magical spot on Portobello Road, a famous street in the Notting Hill district of London where Jimi Hendrix died and U2 was discovered, was the perfect stage to capture the attention of visitors from near and far. These fans from Germany, Italy and Sweden would eventually be the ones to organize and book Ryan's first tour. They asked him to come play back in their home-towns and his answer was, "If you book it, we will come play."

Ryan O'Reilly is not the only artist that used the street as his stage to cultivate a true following and a deep connection with the fans. Stories from the Unknown Tour (which you will hear all about in Chapter 4) prove that great buskers have a special set of performance skills. Billy, one of the filmmakers on the Unknown Tour adventure says, "Some people have the X factor and some don't." Billy and his bud-dies found on the trip across the United States, coast to coast, street performers who had that "X factor" truly have this gift for performing in an engaging way.

Time and time again street performing came up in conver-sation. I asked Josie Dunne, a budding pop singer, "Who do you look up to as a performer for their ability to captivate a crowd?"

Without hesitation, she said Andy Grammer, saying he is "such a show man, his show is almost a work of art." Andy also started on the streets, busking on Santa Monica's Third Street Promenade. At that time he was selling CDs to make rent and now his happy-go-lucky single, "Keep Your Head Up," has put him on the map far beyond his California roots.

The Andy Grammers and Ryan O'Reillys of the streets have the X Factor. It's the lessons of the street that make them an even more powerful performer on the stage. They have found a way to stop people in their tracks amid the business of everyday life to participate in an experience they did not know they were looking for or that they were not actively seeking out. On stage, they have a captive audience of fans and music lovers who sought them out. It's the Andys and Ryans that understand the work it takes to engage people on the street, and they bring that same hustle to the stage.

Ingredients

Stop them in their tracks.

The ability to stop people in their day-to-day life with music on the street is a special gift. People pass by street performers and buskers alike, usually with somewhere they have to be, so there has to be a presence and intention to pull them in. After all, these passersby did not buy a ticket and they were not necessarily looking for a musical experience. So what makes people stop in their tracks? It's a question marketers ask themselves every single day: what can we put in front of consumers that will make them stop in their tracks? Marketers use the Four Ps of Marketing model to help answer this question.

The four P's are:[15]

- Product – What is it that you are offering? A product? A service?
- Price – What does it cost? Money? Time?
- Place – Where is it? Right in front of my face? Or do I have to search for it?
- Promotion – What are the touch points that are building the hype and awareness?

In the case of Ryan O'Reilly here is what is going on:

- Product – live, original music and storytelling.
- Price – free.
- Place – a magical spot on Portobello Road.
- Promotion – self recorded CDs.

This formula worked for Ryan and the crew. How does it translate for other bands on stage?

- Product – live music. Obviously, the better the product, the better traction you will see with the crowd. It takes talent and a story to create the band's image.

- Price – what is it worth? Ryan was strategic in selling CDs not only as promotion but as a sign that the band was worth more than spare change. A higher price can be an indicator of quality and any monetary value leads to a buy-in and commitment from the fan.
- Place – In this book I dive into all sorts of wacky venues. While Ryan was lucky to find a magical spot on Portobello Road, the place for live music can be anywhere with the right intention set. The intention is set with promotion.
- Promotion – it is just as important to communicate what the experience is as much as what it is not. If the show is in a house, then it's not about the lighting effects or the sound quality, it is about storytelling and community experience. That should be communicated. Up and coming musicians spend a lot of time on promotion as do professionals who dedicate their working lives to promotion of top-tier artists, venues, and festivals. Music promotion is a book in and of itself but for the sake of shows that I talk about creating in this book, it is most important that in every touch point with the fan they understand what the experience is about. Even if the creator is still figuring it out, communicate that, "we will figure out together."

CHAPTER 3

LIVE MUSIC IS AT
THE CORNER BAR

———

"Bobby Bare Jr. says it's like playing inside an acoustic guitar," Chris Schuba says as he thinks back on the remarks of artist who played in his bar over the years.

On the corner of Belmont and Southport in the Lakeview neighborhood of Chicago sits Schubas Tavern. A Schlitz sign hangs on the brick building marking the entrance to the 200-capped listening room. Chris Schuba and his brother, Mike, opened the bar in 1989 and their first act on stage was Big Head Todd and the Monsters. At the time, the neighborhood looked very different from today, with prostitutes on the corner and whispering of violence in the street.

The brothers started in the bar business and only held shows on the weekend. However, as weeknights grew quiet, they tapped local talent to draw in patrons. Tuesday nights were dedicated to the 6-part jam band, The Otters. Over their residence at Schubas the band went on to play over 250 shows as the bar quickly evolved to the trusted music showcase room in Chicago.

"The brilliance of the Schuba brothers is they figured out how to create a really comfortable context that honored music and honored the fans and held the musicians in high esteem," said Stuart Rosenberg, fiddler, vocalist, and the one that organized friends to become The Otters, after working with the brothers for years.

Chris said, "It is a very simple concept framed by my experience." After going to his fair share of rock clubs where even the "coolest" bands sound bad, look bad, and feel bad, he decided he would create his own space and flip the ethos. He said, "Let's do it all right. Feed, pay, and honor the music."

The Schubas experience starts for artists the moment they pull up. They are properly fed and given space to do their thing, making bands feel like Schubas is their home away from home on the road. The show the Schubas put on backstage translates to what the bands bring to the main stage.

Fans don't always come to the door in search of the main act. Many times Chris found himself bouncing as passersby asked "Who's playing tonight?" and blindly entered, trusting that in a few years, they will be a somebody. These "somebodies" that played Schubas went on to be stars from Dave Matthews to John Mayer.

On the other side of the spectrum, there were names that fans came for but Chris always reminded them, "I know you bought the ticket for the headliner but don't miss the opener."

The Schuba brothers later bought Lincoln Hall, an old movie theatre turned concert venue. Before they sold to Audioleaf, a local music company that was part of the Greenleaf Companies in Michigan, in April 2015, the two venues were hosting more shows than any other venue in the city.

Many major cities have their own Schubas, a corner of the city carved out for good music and trusted for quality talent. The "Schubas" of the world are often distinguished based on genre and feel from rock to folk to R&B. Yet, with a few bucks burning a hole in a music fan's pocket, this is a place where the doors are always open. It's a consistent place where music lives, music belongs, and music fans are welcome.

Ingredients

A prescribed place.

It is a historic home base. Doors are always open, no invite needed. Schubas, or your local corner bar, is where you come for music and know it will be good. We as human beings associate place with action – church is for prayer, the field is for games, the office is for work, and Schubas is for music. There is a level of comfort and trust that comes with consistency and reliability in a space's use. In this book we discuss the "out of the box venues." There is excitement and adventure that comes with these places but there is a lot of value in the consistency of the corner bar listening room.

CHAPTER 4

LIVE MUSIC IS NOT ABOUT THE CELEBRITIES

———

"We realized that the music industry is really industry and not that much music," said Billy Ferguson, a videographer out of Los Angeles, California.

Billy was on the fast track to success as a filmmaker, shooting videos for top-tier stars of the twenty-first century from Rihanna to Lil Yachty. Mingling with celebrities, Billy quickly learned these artists spent more time prepping for photoshoots and worrying about their social media than actually writing music. To be a musician suddenly seemed to mean being a model, a socialite, and a public figure.

The meaning of being a musician was becoming diluted.

Billy and his co-worker and friend, Jimmy Jimes, grew to appreciate the lesser-known artists they crossed paths with. Equally as talented as some of the big acts, these artists were hungry for the music and art of it all. The two videographers enjoyed working with them as they honed and mastered their craft.

The two were sitting on a golden ticket to stardom with portfolios and contact books rookie videographers would kill for. But they traded in the industry status quo and started working with these up-and-coming artists.

The filmmaking duo dreamt of telling a national story about these unknown artists.

They bought a 36-foot RV and named her Fanny. Fanny received an extreme makeover. She was pimped out in an orange and blue geometric pattern wrapping the exterior. The inside, a time capsule of Americana life on the road, was transformed into a hipper living space and recording studio.

Billy and Jimmy needed a crew to tell their story on the road. They recruited Chris Watson, a Brooklyn singer songwriter living in LA, to be their music supervisor, Zack Djurich to be their musical engineer, and their music-loving buddy Mike Jaeger to be their tour manager and bus driver.

The five set out on the Unknown Tour, a 10-week 20-city run from Los Angeles to New York and back. They hit dive bars, the streets, and house parties in Chicago, Austin, Birmingham, and New Orleans, to name a few, in search of unknown, talented performers. In each city they recorded footage of artists they met in bars, alleyways, and train stations. They invited the most talented back to the RV where, under the guidance of Chris, drummers, rappers, guitarists, and singers laid down a track that would ultimately become a collaborative album of sounds from across the country.

* *

"Making It" Might Not Be The "Big Break" Artist Crave

"Making it" is this loose term that seems to define an artist's success.

There are key milestones artist must hit to "make it" in the traditional sense. It starts with discovery and ends with sold out arena tours and an invite to the set of Saturday Night Live.

The Unknown Tour tested this theory.

They found that most artists just want to play good music and share their story with people, and that is how they define "making it." That is exactly what the Unknown Tour is about – giving a voice and a platform to the unknown. Success to everyone is different and success in our society can cripple true art.

Queue *Strawberries* by Caamp

A song that captures the vulnerability of inviting another person into your life and your story.

On a Wednesday night in March, I found myself being cussed out by Taylor Meier, the lead singer of the band Caamp at the Beachland, an old-school ballroom and Cleveland music destination. He stood alone onstage with his guitar in hand; he had just sung a new song and poured his heart out.

He reminded us all how vulnerable he had just been saying, "How disrespectful that you would fucking talk while I am pouring my heart out up here. You can go fucking talk about work in the lobby."

Taylor invited us into his story in that moment, in a very intimate way stripping himself of his support team, his band. He wanted his story to be heard. Many kids are told "your voice matters." Yet it is the mumbling that rang through the small ballroom, overpowering Taylor's ballad, that tells that little kid in Taylor, "Your voice doesn't matter."

So how can artists share their stories in a way that they are heard? How can Taylor, or any artist for that matter, make it by playing good music and sharing their story if people are going to talk over them?

The Unknown Tour offers one way.

* *

Connection In Vegas

Over the 10 weeks of the tour the five guys would produce a collaborative album with national representation and document their adventures along the way.

First stop—the Vegas strip.

Fanny rolled into town and fit right in among the flashy colors and neon lights that illuminate the gambling capital. In this bold entertainment hub, the adventure was about to begin— but first a trip to the Verizon Wireless store to pick up an internet plug was in order. Little did they know that their lack of internet would lead them to a fellow filmmaker whose brother was a rapper.

Ronny Richeze was the brother's name, a beat boxed by trade and dancer by choice. Ronny was the lucky guest to break in Fanny's recording booth and share stories with the Unknown Tour.

One of the pressing questions of the tour for Billy and the crew was, "Why do musicians do what they do, what lights their fire?"

Ronny says, "I do it for the connection with people. I feel like there is a deeper message. When they hear this or see me dancing they will remember it tomorrow. That is my ideal for success."[16] Ronny recalls how integral dance circles and playing instruments were in Native American communities—a ritual. People are looking to connect, as they have done throughout time through dance and music.

Ronny says, "Let me connect them."

* *

Austin's Musical Brains

Unknown Tour blazed their trail to Austin. There they met Dr. Jim Rose, one of the top local neurosurgeons. Brains by day and trumpet by night — that's how Dr. Rose rolls. He says, "For people to get together and express feelings in a unified fashion, it may be the glue that made civilization possible, maybe even evolution possible. Rhythm. Drums.

Music."[17] That's what makes Dr. Rose tick, similar to Ronny in Las Vegas.

Whaling away on the trumpet, Dr. Rose is doing his part to hold our society together as one can through music.

* *

Feeling the Beat in NYC

In New York the Unknown Crew met a man that goes by Choclatt Jared, who defines himself as a "something from nothing kind of drummer."[18]

He starts playing on buckets and says, "Equipment is great but if you feel the beat and make people feel it, it basically doesn't matter." He's gone from buckets on the street to playing for Aretha Franklin, David Letterman, and Lauren Hill. He also made his way on world tours in Japan.

If you go to a show, "you buy a ticket and after you see the show, the show might be like ahhh," Choclatt Jared sighed in disapproval. "But if you can get someone in their daily life to stop and they watch you and take their time to appreciate you and what you are doing that lets me and my art form know what I am doing is real."[19]

* *

The Unknown Tour proved there is more to music than industry.

Billy said it best, "Music is not all about how many records you sold, how many people come to your shows, how much money you are making off music. Music means more than that to people and the musicians that make the songs have stories to tell that are meaningful to them and those personal stories that come through the music are the stories we want to tell."

Reminded of the meaning behind being an artist by the Unknown Tour, artists and fans alike have the tools to redefine success in music. Beyond money, status, photoshoots, and social media, music is about the story, stories that need to be heard.

Ingredients

Not about the star in the room.

Scottish philosopher Thomas Reid said, "A chain is no stronger than its weakest link,"[20] meaning that if one person fails in the group, the whole group fails. In the music and entertainment scene, fans fail artists with their attention and motives, ultimately failing the whole group.

- Attention – think of the example of a kindergarten class. The teachers are at the front teaching the alphabet when one kid starts playing with scissors and another practically jumps out of their chair. Suddenly there is a chaotic mess of kids so far off target that it seems impossible to reel them back in to the subject at hand. Adults are not all that different. "The tools and technologies that we use every minute of the day are teaching us to constantly be in a 'what else' mindset," says Jocelyn K. Glei. Jocelyn, an author, teacher, speaker and host of Hurry Slowly, a podcast about how people can be more productive, creative, and resilient through the simple act of slowing down.[21] Amid clinking glasses and other social human beings, this "'what else?' mindset" is just an additional barrier that concert-goers have to jump over to slow down and experience the music. If one person is side-tracked, it makes it much easier for the whole group to go flying off the rail, be it in kindergarten class or a concert hall. The Unknown Tour re-invites us to zone in and embrace the unknown artists on our streets and in our local pubs, as well as be attentive to their stories and art.
- Motive – exactly to the point, it's not about the celebrity in the room. When an artist steps on stage they are inviting us into their art and story to create meaning in our

lives— whether they are Bruce Springsteen or Choclatt Jared. In the age of social media where you have to post it or it didn't happen, suddenly people are showing up to see these artists not to experience their art but to prove they did this "cool thing" by snapping a pic. This creates a transactional experience. The motive becomes about the "Who?" and less about the "where, what, when, how" and, most importantly, "why" that capture the essence of the experience that many artists so carefully curate.

The least attentive and disingenuously motivated person in the room influences the entire group. We are called to make room for the unknown and get over the celebrity hype. After all, "making it" for many artists is less about fame and more about the attention and motive of those who engage with their music.

CHAPTER 5

LIVE MUSIC IS ABOUT THE PRESENTATION

"College: a place to learn from the textbooks," says the guy who did college all wrong.

Sure, the focus of college is an academic education that prepares young adults as they transition to the "real world." Textbooks, lectures, and tangents of tenured professors have their place in the learning process. There is power and purpose in the knowledge and wisdom they provide.

However, peer-to-peer learning is often some of the most unique, fruitful learning and growth in one's college experience. With these experiences and friendships, students walk away with a lot more than a diploma to represent their time spent on college campuses and in university halls. That's the kind of stuff that people talk about their whole life – the crazy adventures with friends, the late night talks as they made sense of the world, and the shenanigans one simply does not put on a resume.

At 18 years old Andy Holtgreive packed up for Aquinas College with his new guitar strapped to his back, a gift from his parents. He then made the trek from Kalamazoo to Grand Rapids, Michigan. As fate would have it, the resident advisor (an older student that lived in the dorms with Andy and other freshman serving as a "big brother" in their transition to college), Christian, was a musician and Andy's new neighbor. He wrote lyrics, played guitar, and, in true 90s fashion, recorded music on eight tracks.

Andy found a friend and teacher in his RA, Christian.

Their jam sessions quickly evolved into writing lessons. Andy learned to write his first song and between freshman and sophomore year had written a handful of songs to add to his repertoire.

Returning for sophomore year, Andy and Christian formed a band they called Plumber Butt with another buddy,

Vince. Vince lived off campus in a community with some students working on a year-long service project and proposed that Plumber Butt play a show in their living room, with no amplification and no frills.

"It was insane and it was fun," Andy recalls. They did blues riffs, covers and originals. It was then that Andy "got the bug" – he loved being in front of people, acting silly, and playing music. They packed 100 students into the room like sardines and played five shows over the course of that year.

Blues Brothers was Plumber Butt's 101 class in performance. They were obsessed, Andy says. He adds, "We watched that movie 10 times a week."

> **Queue *Everybody Needs Somebody to Love* by The Blues Brothers**

Their favorite scene was in the Soul Food Café after Elwood and Jake, the Blues Brothers, returned from a show in the not so glamorous Joliet Correctional Center. They reminisce on shows past with Matt Murphy, the cook at the café and an old band member.

Jake turns to Matt and says, "Matt, me and Elwood, we're putting the band back together. We need you and Blue Lou."

While Matt's wife shoots him the stink eye, he responds to Jake saying, "Oh man, don't talk that way around here. My old lady, she'd kill me."

Elwood turns to Mrs. Murphy in hopes of knocking some sense into her. He says, "Ma'am, you have to understand. This is bigger than any domestic problems you might be experiencing."[22]

Inspired by *Blues Brothers* in more ways than one, the band formerly known as "Plumber Butt," hit center stage junior year on homecoming weekend in front of 600 people under their new name, "Bigger Than Any Domestic Problem You May Be Experiencing." In true Blues Brothers fashion, their homecoming set was all about the drama and the presentation. With briefcases and handcuffs they walked onstage and performed their own kind of *Blues Brothers* spoof.

They started to create a name for themselves on Aquinas's campus opening for buddies at the local bar, Martinis. They shortened their name to "Domestic Problems" and pulled together a set mainly of covers and about a third of which were originals that Andy had written. They were all the rage as friends and fans chattered, "Hey let's go see Andy, Billy, and Christain play," around campus.

With no formal experience and training outside of their *Blue Brothers* crash course, Andy shares, "It wasn't really about the music, it was just about the exchange, the interaction, people just having fun, not taking anything too seriously and having a good time."

The Martini's bar owner saw the energy they brought to the stage and the following they cultivated, he did not care how they sounded. The bar owner had a proposition, "Why don't you guys come back next week? You keep playing on Wednesday nights, I'll pay you a beer."

As the new Martini's resident band, they started playing more shows, learning more songs, and Andy started writing more music. As time passed, they took their talents from their college hang out to local venues as headliners.

* *

They happened to be in the right place at the right time.

In 1997 there was a swell around local music in Western Michigan with songs like "The Freshman" by Verve Pipe at the pinnacle of this musical buzz. Many thought Grand Rapids was on the fast track to be the next music hot spot.

"There was a real live, legitimate music scene of original music that the community came out and supported because, I think, the Verve Pipe was getting all this national attention," Andy recalls. "Once they got signed by RCA, it brought more attention to the local music scene." RCA is a major American electronics company, which was founded as the Radio Corporation of America that signed talent from Elvis Presley to the Backstreet Boys.

In the wave of this momentum, in 1997, Domestic Problems released their second album "Play." Two years out of college, Andy made music his full time gig. Domestic Problems got hooked up with the National Association of Campus Activities (NACA), which sent them on a tour to 30 cities. In Texas, Arkansas, Louisiana, and Oklahoma they played college campuses and local dive bars. College campuses offered the budgets that launched the band to make music their full-time gig and dive bars allowed them to hit 200 shows a year.

Domestic Problems entered a contest to play HORDE Tour (Horizons of Rock Developing Everywhere), a traveling summer rock music festival that started in 1992. In 1997, Domestic Problems won a spot to play three shows in Detroit, Michigan, Scranton and Pittsburgh, Pennsylvania. Neil Young and Crazy Horse, Primus, Big Head Todd and The Monsters, and Toad The Wet Sprocket were among a few of the names that Domestic Problems shared the festival grounds with. Playing the first set of the day on the second stage, Andy and Domestic Problems had the same access pass to the festival as Neil Young. A major win to be in the presence of incredible star power, Andy said, "We felt like this is it, we're making our way."

* *

Not every show was as noteworthy as the HORDE tour.

The underbelly of the excitement of sold out shows and big name lineups was playing shows at Q Bar in Iowa City for 10 people or the stadium at Miami, Ohio for a crowd of five. Andy always said in these situations, "We have got to play like there's 5,000 people here. Whether there's five or 5,000 should make no difference. We got to bring it on."

Sometimes these more "intimate shows," as Andy jokingly called them, gave Domestic Problems the time to hone their craft. The experience reveals the lesson to be "committed to what you're doing and not reliant upon who you were doing it for necessarily," Andy remarks.

Andy would open to the crowd by saying, "We promise whatever energy you give back to us, we'll kick it back to you 10 times. It's an exchange."

Math and science lead us to believe that the more people in the room = more energy.

Andy notes, "You can be in front of 1,500 people and they could care less about you and that sucks. But, it's the amount of attention and intention that's being exchanged that really makes a difference on the quality of that live show." A room of 10 giving an artist undivided attention is more powerful and rewarding than an arena full of disinterested fans talking louder than the band is playing over booming speaker systems.

When Andy dreams up his ideal show as an artist, after five years of touring full time and 25 years of playing with his college buddies in Domestic Problems, he thinks of a time "when you can connect and feel that connection. You probably have that ability to connect in a smaller, more intimate setting, that's what I want. I want people that are there because they want to see music and they're paying attention to it."

* *

Attention is an invaluable currency to artists, one that cannot be forced or bought.

Whether it is nostalgic reunion tours with college friends and family filling the crowd or opening for Rustic Root at the Fox Theatre and winning the crowd and the band over, mutually engaging in the experience with the crowd is what Andy aspires to.

Andy walked away with much more than a diploma to credit his time at Aquinas College. He graduated with new musical skills, a band, and a community rooted in Grand Rapids that launched him into a musical career with fans eagerly awaiting reunion shows to this day. The Blues Brothers were on a "mission from God," as they fought to save the orphanage the brothers grew up in from closing.

Andy is on his own mission, to generate an exchange with a live crowd. It is the attention of the crowd, the excitement to be there for music, and the intention of the artist, to perform and connect, that creates an energizing experience.

Ingredients

Exchange of Energy

Domestic Problems gave back 10 times the energy that the audience radiated. If the audience did not give energy, the band still brought it and then some. It is not about the attention of the crowd but intention of the musicians. More intention from the musicians inspires more intention from the crowd. You don't have to be the best musicians in the world to execute this. If you have fun performing, the crowd will have fun too. Channel your inner Blues Brother. Presentation is the name of the game.

CHAPTER 6

LIVE MUSIC CAN BE D.I.Y. AND DONE RIGHT

House shows are no new concept. History has it that Mozart himself threw a mean house show back in the day, banging away on the keys.

Before recorded music, on eight tracks, cassettes, Walkmans, records, CDs, iPods, and Spotify, the only way to hear music was live. People played around campfires, held balls, and, yes, played live music for friends in their living rooms. Groups like Sofar Sounds emerged and have legitimized the live music that has been playing in people's homes for years (we will get to them in Chapter 8). Other companies like Airbnb

Music, Little Concerts and Back Door are doing the same, bringing live music into intimate spaces, but on different scales and in their own fashion. These platforms have gotten creative and put shows on not only in homes but in any space that is willing to give artists the stage, or in many cases just a small corner of their loft, restaurant, boat deck, or even a barber shop.

Brett Newski,an artist who plays "good proper midwest indie rock" according to Matthew Logan Vasquez of Delta Spirit, is among the artist playing shows at strange, "outside-the-box" venues. On his own time and on his own terms, Brett has gone far beyond homes and seemingly unconventional spaces that traditional promoters and even the Sofar Sounds platform have set up for artists and fans to experience live music. Known by many to be the first band ever kicked out of a Wal-Mart for playing an illegal show, D.I.Y. is truly the name of the game for Brett.

"On a lazy summer Saturday, my drummer Spatola and I decided it was time we made our Wal-Mart debut, playing an impromptu show for unsuspecting shoppers at America's behemoth buying warehouse," Brett said. "We bum rushed through the entrance and blasted into the tune 'Can't Get Enough.'"

> **Queue *Can't Get Enough* by Brett Newski**
>
> *It's great to see you're living like you mean it*
> *I want to mean it too*

Some shoppers stopped to take a Snapchat or share a chuckle as they milled about doing whatever one does in a Milwaukee Wal-Mart. One man felt the music move right through him, put a pep in his step, and danced with Brett and Spatola through the Vitamin aisle.

But, turns out the Wal-Mart staff could get enough of Brett.

"Sorry guys, we gotta run a business here," one of the Wal-Mart employees said, breaking the bad news to Brett.[23]

* *

In 2016 Brett traveled to four continents and played 150 shows. In between playing classic music venues, big theaters with 1000 people and living room shows with 12 people, he managed to do, what he coins, "The Weirdest Venues in the World Tour."

People were not the only guests at his show in a toolshed in South Germany. Chickens and goats also participated in Brett's singalongs, "squawking" and "bleating" away.

A homeless spell in Prague led Brett to find refuge at night on children's nap pads. Every good story starts with, "I have a friend of a friend." Well, this "friend of a friend" happened to be a kindergarten teacher who cut a deal with Brett. The nap pads were all his at night if he would play a rocking show for tots by day.

Would you put a music venue under a train? Me either. The train literally rocked the house in Vienna, Austria where Brett played a tiny bohemian venue that fit only about 60 people. It sounds like a cool, trendy venue in theory but Brett says, "This was perhaps the worst show of the year."

In the spirit of collaboration, Brett worked with local promoters around the world to play more outlandish spaces. He played in a 200-year-old attic, a vintage furniture shop, the top of a mountain in Appenzell, Switzerland, a bakery, and if you thought things couldn't get weirder, in a MONA museum in Hobart, Tasmania next to a wall of hundreds of plaster cast vaginas.

Amongst all the weirdness there is a show that sticks out.

"I played a show in an alleyway in Central Saigon, Vietnam to just local people who didn't speak English. That was pretty trippy." There was a little girl who was deaf that worked at a local business. She came out while Brett played and he recalls, "She would come up and put her hand on the end of the guitar so she could feel the vibrations and she would just freak out with joy."

* *

Queue *D.I.Y.* by Brett Newski

Brett wrote a song about the D.I.Y. lifestyle he has chosen after countless shows getting the stink eye, people talking over his music, and spilling beer on him mid-set – times when the audience was not as starstruck as the young girl in Saigon. "I am D.I.Y., I am punk as fuck. I don't need your money, I don't want your love," he sings in the chorus of "D.I.Y."

"It's a lot more hours going the D.I.Y. route," Brett points out. But, on the other hand, "going the industry route, you just have a lot more hands in your pockets."

In traditional venues artists pay the club, the agent, the manager, the publicist, sounds guys and everyone who puts their fingers on your hour and a half set. With the D.I.Y. approach, the middleman is cut out. Sure, the artist takes on a lot of the workload but they reap a lot of the reward at the end of the day.

Go D.I.Y. and keep it weird, wonderful, and punk as fuck.

Ingredients

Weird and Wonderful

Go somewhere uncharted whether it is Wal-Mart, a mountaintop, a tool shed, or a museum filled with plaster cast vaginas. The weirder the place that an artist invites a crowd into, the more adventurous the crowd. They are taking a leap of faith to go somewhere different so they must be in it for the core of the event, the music. Adventure does not have to mean jumping out a plane or hang gliding through the Alps. According to experts, adventure is about one's mindset, looking at every day with a sense of possibility.[24] It's looking at Wal-Mart or mountaintop or toolshed and seeing it as an opportunity to be a music venue. Fans must move into this mindset, buy into the possibility of these weird venues and meet artists where they are at a given moment in time.

CHAPTER 7

LIVE MUSIC CAN BE A LEGITIMIZED HOUSE PARTY

"It's sort of felt like I was a bit like a therapist or a career counselor," Laura Simpson jokes as her office became a venue for musicians' vent sessions.

Laura was working for a nonprofit Music Nova Scotia that supports artists in the business aspects of their career. In fact, every province in Canada has a nonprofit that helps musicians navigate all the logistics beyond the music. In her seven years as Communication and Membership Coordinator and then Funding Programs Officer, her office became the perfect space for musicians to vent about their pains in the industry.

Laura had been a sounding board for musicians long before she had a title to prove it.

She grew up on all-age concerts in Halifax, Nova Scotia and found dear friends in the musicians whose music became the soundtrack to her youth. She got frustrated when she saw the pain her friends experienced working with certain venues and was an advocate for her friends' rights from the get-go, making sure the money stayed in their pockets rather than those of the venues or the promoters.

When Laura and her husband Scott bought an abandoned nineteenth century house in North Halifax, they knew they wanted to host concerts in it as they transformed it into a home. "The Syrup Factory," they called it, after the small cordial-making factory that used to be there.

Laura said, "I knew my heart was in doing live presentations." So her side hustle began at the Syrup Factory solving a problem for the artist, community members, and herself.

- For the artist – the artists who were venting in her office now had a platform to share their talents where they walked away with 100% of the profits in their pockets.

- For community members – the friends who were always asking Laura, as their resident music guru, "Well who should I listen to?" Laura invited them into her home and introduced them to new music.
- For herself – a mother of two, Laura jokes, "I had babies and I couldn't go out as much." So what did she do? Brought the entertainment to her living room.

"I remember feeling afraid that people would go on the second floor to where my children were sleeping," she recalled, but nothing ever happened. Now her kids are part of the production; they help by introducing all the shows and working the door, fully immersed in the experience.

* *

"Wait, is this a house?" curious patrons of the Syrup Factory have asked.

"Yeah, it's my house," Laura responds.

"Wait, you live here?" They answer in disbelief, "I'm so sorry."

"No, no, I invited you."

In shaking up the way many people are currently experiencing music— traditionally in corner bars, concert venues, and festival grounds— Laura has been tasked to figure out how to normalize this familiar yet unfamiliar space.

It starts with logistics.

A variety of seating is set up around the room for those who like to experience the show up close, in the kitchen, and on the stairs. This customizable space allows patrons to experience the music in their own way and in their own space. They ask for names rather than tickets at the door, receiving people as guests, not as numbers. Before the event, they communicate as much as possible about the experience to provide clarity from parking to the food at the event. When Laura breaks hospitality down she says, "My husband and I really like hosting anyway, so we've kind of just treated everybody like they were a friend and that continues to be the approach."

Laura envisioned Syrup Factories all over the world. So, she co-founded Side Door in 2017 as a way "to empower people to create their own communities, just in the same way that I did in my own little part of Halifax," she says.

Laura and her co-founder Dan Mangan, a singer songwriter, have democratized the entertainment industry. They are giving audiences the direct access to book artists in their own spaces and artists fair and direct pay from contracts. Only

10% of the money goes to Side Door and the artist and host can negotiate the remaining 90%, with a max of 40% for the host.

This is no "one size fits all." Hosts log onto the platform and create a profile that expresses their musical interest. Taking into consideration the preferences and behaviors of hosts, Side Door serves as the matchmaker to artists, curating in a way that makes sense for both parties. From there, Side Door takes a step back. They have policies for hosts on how to make their space safe and respectful but beyond that, the hosts have creative control.

"The measure of success is such a moving target for artists and there's a whole set of things that they think that they should do because they're told that that's important." Laura says, "Then there's what they really want to do, which in most cases is just get their work heard and appreciated."

Laura has made it easier for artists to connect with hosts and to be heard and appreciated, doing what they want to do not what they should do. Syrup Factory and Side Door offer an authentic showcase for artists and a space to capture community.

Ingredients

Treat everyone like a friend

For hosts, this is hospitality 101. It is weird to walk into a stranger's home. The faster you become friends, the more comfortable it will feel. It's the simple things that introduce this sort of a friendship— like asking for a name at the door, not a ticket. People want to be recognized as a unique individual rather than a number, so treat them like one.

The tools and the freedom

Side Door provides the connections for artists and guidelines for basic safety and respect in the space for hosts and guests. The rest is up to the creative genius of the artists and the hosts to capture a piece of their community. Artists and the venue owners are the names on the bill at the end of the day, so they are given the freedom to design the show. However, it's daunting to do something all on your own and Side Door's value proposition is that they are the experts and resources in the creation process.

CHAPTER 8

LIVE MUSIC IS HYPER LOCAL WITH GLOBAL CONNECTIONS

In 2009, Rafe Offer went to see Friendly Fires in the SOHO neighborhood of London. As Rafe tells the story, phones were out, beer bottles were clinking and there was a room full of people deep in conversations about anything but the show they had come to see. Instead of being the main event, the music was background noise.

It was in that moment that he turned to his two friends, Rocky Start (yes, you read that right) and David Alexander, and they agreed, "This is not ok, music should be about a connection and we don't feel like we are connecting with the band." [25] With all these barriers, it felt as though the concert they had come to see was not the musical, human-centric experience they craved.

"It is absolutely soul-destroying to be singing to people who are not really attentive," said David, an up-and-coming artist.[26]

Rafe, Rocky and David, all music junkies in their own right, looked to address the disappointment they were feeling in the concert experience.

"Songs from a room."

That was their solution, the new concept they dreamt up. It was by no means radical. For generations people have hosted house concerts but in that moment, this idea was new to them.

They gave the idea a shot it in North London. David played a show for eight people in his own living room. They sat on the floor and in the stark silence they heard the clicking of the clock's arms, the beat as time passed. A transformative experience for the three men, the performance was very different than the noisy London bar. Creating this environment for musical connection became a hobby for the trio.

The word spread about these intimate gigs. When they put on their third show in Regents Park, there was a line down the block of music lovers frustrated with their experiences in traditional venues who wanted to try something new. This idea of "songs from a room" manifested into something bigger as newfound fans of the concept adapted it to make it more their own, bringing their own drinks, channeling their talents to take photos and videos of the shows, and offering up unique spaces.

That is Sofar Sounds.

* *

Word spread to L.A. Rafe got a call one day from a woman named Casey, a music-lover following Sofar from California. She wanted to host one of these shows. Rafe thought, "Well it is just a house show, yes you can."

But Casey responded, "No you don't understand, we want to join your community. We want to know how you are doing it and we want to connect." [27]

Sofar created some rules that Casey and others could follow to host a Sofar in their city. The rules are to be alive, be human, and please pay attention to the music. With these rules in place, a movement began.

To L.A. and Beyond

Sofar has scaled to reach over 400 cities worldwide and turns anything from a living room to a ski jump into a venue for an intimate gig with about 100 people. Every lineup is specially curated to give audiences a diverse show and an element of surprise upon arrival. Twenty-four hours before the gig, a secret address is shared with guests and they are left wondering who the musical talent is going to be. On a given night guests might see an R&B soul-filled group followed by a singer songwriter with a country twang followed by a spoken word poet.

The spontaneous and alternative nature of these secret gigs might be misinterpreted as a place for a "weird millennial hipster kind of person," but as current Regional Director of Operation Matt Brooks shares, Sofar is not for one archetype. Rather, "every kind of person goes to Sofar, it's all around the world."

He continues to say, "I think what's special [about] Sofar is you can meet people that have so many different interests, passions, career paths and ways of life but this simple idea of listening to music can bring us together."

Matt was a student at Butler in Indianapolis when he stumbled across Sofar's YouTube page. He was bummed to find

Sofar was not in Indianapolis so he conducted an interview for Do 317, a local resource that connects community members to the hottest events and happenings, to start a Sofar in Indianapolis. After looking for the right person to create Sofar Indianapolis, he realized he could be the one to do it. He was the one to do it.

Matt attended his first show on a trip back home to Chicago at an airy studio space. After being immersed in a night of tunes with Sofar, he left feeling like he "had discovered the best kept secret in the city."

He brought this little secret back to Indianapolis, built a team of close friends around the city to run the gigs and started hosting shows in May 2016. He elevated the music scene in Indy and brought music fans together in an intentional community. Upon graduation he took his talents to Chicago where he was hired as the Sofar City Director. But, before hitting the ground running in his hometown, he took a trip overseas to see family.

During a quick, 20-hour layover in Athens, Matt hoped to sneak in a Sofar show. Times didn't line up so Matt reached out to the Sofar Athens team asking for recommendations of things to do as a music lover and in the Sofar spirit. Instead of giving recommendations they said, "What hotel are you at? We will meet you there at 6."

Sure enough, at 6 o'clock Matt was joined by a band of Greeks greeting him with warm hugs. An experience like no other, Matt learned "you have friends and community wherever you go."

Back in the prideful city of Chicago, Matt began to design experiences for bands and music fans capturing an element of warmth that he experienced from the Greek Sofar community. In Chicago, a city "where they fly their flag higher than the American flag," it didn't take big name talent or being at the top of the Sears Tower to create magic. Matt directed a show at his dream venue, the Garfield Park Conservatory and yes, the Skydeck at the Sears Tower, yet he kept coming back to shows held in loft apartments as some of his favorites.

"It is about the host more than the space," Matt shared. It is the couple in a ten-story apartment with two golden retrievers that greets guests at the door with appetizers they have prepared that cultivate the Sofar spirit at its finest.

The community that Rafe has inspired worldwide and Matt has created in Indianapolis, Chicago, and now in his new role as Regional Director of Operations in Boston offers thousands of special intimate moments globally every month.

* *

It's moments like this that define Sofar

At a gig in New York City in the Bowery neighborhood on the first floor the door was left open a crack. After the first performance, a homeless man wandered in. He sat down, he smelled a little, but no one minded, he was just as attentive as anyone else. This was in the early days of Sofar, before ticketing. So at the end of the show, a hat was passed around to collect some loose change to support the Sofar efforts. People threw in five, maybe ten dollars as they got up to leave. This homeless man dug deep into his pocket and pulled out a twenty dollar bill. Without hesitation he threw it into the hat and walked out the door. A volunteer chased him down to thank him for his generous donation and he responded, "No, thank you. Thank you for creating a community of people together who made me feel so welcomed." This man was a musician all his life and understood how special it was to perform in a space that sacred. [28]

This man is not the only one who felt part of a larger community and deeper purpose at Sofar. In Istanbul, a single man and women sit down next to one another. They chat and exchange numbers. A year later, Sam got in touch with the Sofar team in Milan right before he and his girlfriend headed there to visit for a holiday. In a room full of strangers Sam got down on one knee and proposed to his girlfriend. They shared a transformative life experience in the Sofar space.

A frustration in a London bar and a house show of just eight people has snowballed into a community-driven music movement around the world.

Artists are vulnerable when they play their music in its most raw form.

Hosts open their doors and express radical hospitality.

Rafe, Matt, city directors, and volunteers around the world set the stage for community that allows a homeless man in NYC to feel accepted, as well as connects Sam and his now wife wherever in the world they attend a Sofar show.

Here you see the Sofar rules in action— to be alive and to be human.

Ingredients

Community wherever you go.

For Sofar is global. It is through a ritual of gathering, a set of rules that serve as a manifesto, and in tradition that a sense of familiarity is fostered whether in London, L.A., New York or Oslo. There is a parallel between Sofar and global religious communities. Take Catholicism for example. For many devoted Catholics, when they travel they desire to visit the local church and experience its Mass. While each church is unique and holds its own identity, there is a level of sameness in the rituals. The rituals of Mass, Communion and the sacraments look the same. The spoken and sung prayer— while in different languages— tells the same message. Just as a guest can walk into a church with an expectation of what they are about to experience, they can walk into a Sofar show and do the same. There is a ritual in which the MC invites guests in and introduces artists. There is music, a point of common interest and way of communication for all in the room. With this global community, there is power and pride knowing that this musical immersion happening in NYC is also simultaneously happening in some of the 400 cities around the world. Being part of a group experiencing "songs from a room" is being part of a larger collective and story.

CHAPTER 9

LIVE MUSIC IS SO MUCH MORE THAN A "CONCERT"

Brian Chesky, Joe Gebbia, and Nathan Blecharczyk were three guys living in San Francisco who quit their jobs, and wanted to be entrepreneurs. In 2008, they got a notice from their landlord warning that rent had gone up 25 percent. On the verge of getting evicted they had to find a way to save their apartment. They saw a sold out design conference passing through San Francisco as an opportunity for them to make some extra cash by turning their living room into a bed and breakfast. They designed airbedandbreakfast.com where they listed three airbeds in their living room for $80 during the design conference. They picked the guests up from the airport, showed them around San Francisco and made them feel at home. It was an unconventional concept they had created; they invited strangers into their home and their most intimate spaces. What they created went against everything they learned as kids: you are not supposed to trust strangers. Don't talk to them, don't get too close to them, and definitely don't go into your home with them.

The trio defied childhood lessons finding trust, friendship, and eventually a global company, with strangers.

In 2008 they worked to scale this concept, to give people access to one another's homes nearby and in faraway places. They called it Airbnb.

Their journey launching Airbnb was no walk in the park – they sold cereal to fund their business and were told by top investors in Silicon Valley "this is crazy," "this is weird," and "this is never going to work at scale.'"

Brian, Joe, and Nathan opened their apartment, their home, ten years ago and shared their story with guests. They now give people in 81,000 cities and 191 countries around the world the platform to open their own homes and share their own stories. Needless to say the privately owned company scaled pretty well – take that Silicon Valley! Over five million unique places to stay are listed on the Airbnb "Homes" platform and there are over 15,000 unique, handcrafted activities curated by locals on the Airbnb Experience platform.

A people-to-people platform at the core, Airbnb's motto is "belong anywhere."

Airbnb Experience of Belonging

Airbnb Experiences was launched in November 2016 to provide "unprecedented access and deep insights into communities and places that you wouldn't otherwise come across," according to Airbnb's website.[29] They initially launched in 12 cities. The first experiences included adventures like truffle hunting in Tuscany and exploring the grime music scene in London. In the past two years, local hosts have curated experiences in over 1,000 markets around the world.

On the platform, private concerts started popping up in the Louvre in Paris and independent artists started inviting guests into live studio sessions in New York City. Music naturally took prominence in Experiences as one of the strongest beats, as it exemplified local culture, character, and identity. In August 2017, the Airbnb founders Brian, Joe, and Nathan, saw they were carving out a special niche in the music experience. They brought on James Beshara, former Head of Social Travel at Airbnb, to lead a team into this new foray, Airbnb Music.

In April 2018, Airbnb Music officially launched, bringing local live music experiences to customers worldwide in an Airbnb style. James describes the core mission of Airbnb Music as "facilitating human connection and hopefully, with amazing experiences, a transformation through that connection."

Airbnb could have chosen to take a deep dive into any of the niche experiences listed on their platform, from sports to history to food or any other facet of the arts. However, there is something special about music, James shared, so that is where they started. He says, "Music is this universal language that you could come to San Francisco from China, not speak a lick of English and still enjoy a night of that."

Tapping into this universal language, James describes how Airbnb has created "small intimate concerts that can help travelers and locals discover amazing artists in the city in which they're traveling or living in a much better way than large concerts or a much better way than really almost any other type of thing we could think of around local art."

Shows are as small as 20 and cap at 100. Houseboats, churches, and rooftops have been transformed into center stage in 40 cities.

AFROHAUSE Brunch – one part dance hall, one part block party

For James, it's AFROHAUSE Brunch in Los Angeles California that he raves about, saying it was "perhaps one of my favorites, if not my favorite concert I've ever been to."

"It really flips the conventional definition of a concert on its head," James shares. The WAV, an artist collective and the pioneers of Afrobeats and Afrotrap in L.A., has transformed an empty retail space in the Inglewood neighborhood into a musical journey across the diaspora they call AFROHAUS Brunch. Inglewood is historically an unsafe neighborhood that no tourists are flocking to. However, AFROHAUS Brunch "is pulling in tourists from around the world, hundreds of them every month to see everything from R&B to slam poetry to Coldplay covers all while you get to eat brunch and soul food cooked by locals."

James isn't the only one raving about this cultural experience. AFROHAUS Brunch holds a 4.7 star rating and over 180 golden reviews from attendees. Tara wrote after her visit in August 2018, "it is difficult to describe the beauty that came together in that space. So many different people and cultures came together to celebrate music. I danced all my cares away and had an amazing time sharing the space with everyone."[30]

Other guests rave about the welcoming energy that emanated from the hosts as they invited them into their space in Inglewood. Liza, an attendee in August 2018, writes, "I felt we were all made to feel that the journey is experienced and shared together while watching the most incredible talent, amazing music, heartfelt performances, dope MC's, DJ's and Hosts."[31]

The culmination of food, painting, poets, and musical performances in a backyard garden creates an amazing atmosphere. Not to mention, this is a BYOB event and Melissa found when she attended in August 2018, this aspect only added to the experience. She said, "That's just another form of community, everyone sharing what they had for the sake of the vibe."[32]

This unbelievable mix of concepts is hard to classify. What do you call an afternoon with strangers that is one part dance hall, one part block party with music, art, and food?

For James, the word "concert" doesn't cut it. In fact he says, "There isn't a name that really does it justice."

Airbnb Music encourages creation of "concerts" unique to the host and their community.

They created the space for artist collectives like The WAV to showcase their most authentic selves and connect to travelers and locals alike with AFROHAUS. With Airbnb Music Experiences, the doors are open to travelers from 10,000 miles away to be a part of a new community, even if it is only for a few hours. Bianca wrote after attending AFROHAUS Brunch, "I have never felt such a personal connection with a better group of strangers."[33]

* * *

Through music, James and his team at Airbnb are creating the vehicle for people like Bianca and the 20,000 Airbnb Music monthly attendees to "belong anywhere." Sure, 20,000 attendees might not sound like much; Madison Square Garden can hold 20,000 in a given night. The company is not trying to compete with stadium tours and major festivals. Their value proposition is the intimacy, digging to the root of community and connection through music. Airbnb in both their Homes and Experience sectors has capitalized on sharing intimate space and creating the feeling of belonging. Whether you call it a concert or not, Airbnb Music has integrated community into live music experiences in a unique, memorable way.

Ingredients

Live like a local – lean into the local culture.

That's what AFROHAUS Brunch does. It is through the mixing of media and through unapologetic authenticity to L.A. and the afrobeats sound that AFROHAUS Brunch is on the map as a to-do for music lovers in L.A. Placed in Inglewood, the experience offers a glimpse into an L.A. often unseen by tourists and even the locals. Maybe the word "concert" doesn't encapsulate all that AFROHAUS Brunch embodies. However, rich themes of L.A. and afrobeat culture are showcased through music, art, dance, food, and stories inviting people in to live like a local.

CHAPTER 10

LIVE MUSIC CONNECTS PAST, PRESENT AND FUTURE

On the shore of Lake Erie in Cleveland, Ohio, a glass building resembling a pyramid stands atop years of historical music archives. The Rock and Roll Hall of Fame recognizes and archives the history of the most influential musicians, artists, producers, engineers, and figures of rock and roll.

"Here at the Rock and Roll Hall of Fame we preserve and exhibit the artifacts that tell the stories of our lives," says Greg Harris, the CEO of the Rock and Roll Hall of Fame.

"And rock and roll connects all of us. These stories are our stories. By helping us preserve these artifacts, you help us preserve your story right here at the Rock and Roll Hall of Fame."[34]

The Rock Hall is connecting the past with the present. The team connects what they are doing now to what was happening 10 years ago, 20 years ago, and even 50 years ago. When you look at an artist like Alabama Shakes or Brittany Howard, you see their unique rhythms and spiritual lyrics influenced by Sister Rosetta Tharpe, a gospel singer, songwriter, and recording artist hot in the 1930s and 1940s who was a precursor to the era of rock and roll.

There is a chain effect of artists influencing one another. The Rock Hall pulls these pieces of the musical, historical equation into exhibits and programming, creating a more active experience rather than a presentation. The question is then: who is going to be influenced by Alabama Shakes and Brittany Howard, continuing to modernize and revolutionize the intersection of gospel and rock and roll music?

The Rock Hall brings these musical timelines to life through exhibits and a series of events that happen year-round, educating visitors on the past and influencing the future. Events pick up in the summer months during Rock Hall Live! On the sprawling, circular brick plaza, the Rock Hall teams up with PNC Bank to bring a number of events, many of which are free, to the general public. These events can be broken up into tiers based on levels of engagement and revenue.

Bottom Tier

On the bottom level you find recurring events like Rock Hall Live! Lunch by the Lake where local artists set up for workers' lunch break midday on Wednesdays, Thursdays, and Fridays, and Summer in the City on Wednesday nights. This past summer of 2018, Summer in the City showcased exceptional female-fronted bands in July and August for what was coined Women Who Rock. These events are casual for people to pop in and experience a glimpse of what the Rock Hall has to offer. They set the tone for the daily Rock Hall experience.

Middle Tier

On the middle tier you will find events like Rock and Recovery, a larger summer event but one that doesn't cost a lot to produce and does not require much programming. Rock and Recovery was a partnership and plaza activation event that took place in the summer of 2018 with Recovery Resource, a Cleveland nonprofit and community-based behavioral healthcare organization that helps people triumph over mental illness, alcoholism, drug and other addictions. Rock & Recovery is a radio channel that mixes music with positive messaging for those in recovery. Ricky Byrd, formally a member of Joan Jett & The Blackhearts, a Rock Hall inductee who is open about his road to recovery, was the frontman talent for the event. He has written an album called "Clean Getaway" about his challenge with sobriety and attends group counseling regularly. For this event, Ricky led a song-writing circle and engaged in intimate conversation on the topic of recovery with other friends and music lovers. Music was the language, the vehicle, which initiated the conversation about recovery. It was with the added elements of mindfulness and storytelling that supported and brought this community together.

Top Tier

On the top tier you will find a capstone or pinnacle event that is "crazy, intense, amazing, incredible, all hands on deck," as Kathryn Clusman, manager of community and family programs, explains. It is an in-your-face, all day extravaganza – it is Klipsch Fest. Klipsch is a speaker, headphones and home audio company that sponsors the music fest annually at the Rock Hall in order to "preserve and celebrate the live music experience." The 2018 Klipsch Fest was headlined by nationally touring punk rock band Social Distortion. Leading up to the main act, which was free with admission to the museum, there were DJ sets and a live performance from a number of local and touring bands.

At every level of events you see live music, which seems obvious as you are reading a book about live music experience and we are talking about one of the most iconic music museum destinations. As Zoe Ingram, the strategic project manager at Rock Hall, points out, you "can't imitate music. It has to be." It has to be real. It has to be present. It has to be live. It can't be recreated or imitated.

When we take a look at the added elements that influence the way patrons and rockers experience the music, we see there is a great level of attention and detail that the Rock Hall addresses. On the first tier you see the Rock Hall strategically produce the onstage "Women Who Rock" Summer in the City series while they simultaneously highlight female rock stars in the museum hall exhibits. With Rock and Recovery, the partnerships that the Rock Hall forms support their mission. At the top you see all the Rock Hall is, was and will be come to life in Klipshfest. Like a puzzle, everything fits together. By latching different pieces together, success will come to Rock Hall.

Defining Success

The definition of "success" looks different for each of these events as they each have their niche target. The Rock Hall recognizes that people come visit them for different reasons. Some come for a nostalgic journey down memory lane while others come to check the Rock Hall off their bucket list as they play tourist in Cleveland. Many pay a visit as a music enthusiast or as a professional in the industry while others simply visit because family or friends wanted them to join. The Rock Hall has to cater to the number of different motives that bring people to their space while still staying authentic to their mission.

When defining level of success in events, Kathryn asks questions like, "Are you reaching an audience you have reached before? Are you reaching people who are going to come back? Are you reaching people who are going to talk about it? Are you reaching people at all? Maybe your event numbers weren't high, but they're the best damn time." Setting goals to reach new audiences, keep people coming back and providing kickass, memorable experiences keeps the Rock Hall motivated and moving forward. However, tt is important to keep in mind that sometimes the data is not representative of the experience of it self and take a step back. The numbers of an event might not meet quota but the quality of the experience speaks volumes for those who did attend.

Collaboration is Key

It is with this same, strategic lens that the Rock Hall has learned to collaborate internally and maximize on events happening locally. When major artists make their way through town, the Rock Hall doesn't miss a beat. Billy Joel played a sold out show at The Quicken Loans Arena, so the Rock Hall played his music and did a pop-up exhibit with artifacts of his the day of the show.

When Taylor Swift played down the street at FirstEnergy Stadium, Rock Hall hosted Taylegate, a free event on the plaza with music, access to a bar, food, and bathrooms. Upwards of 100,000 people are passing the plaza making the Rock Hall grounds the perfect stop off. Kiss FM set up a red carpet and photo booth and gave away free tickets. The Accidentals, a young hip band with some crossover with Taylor's fans but with a little more rock to them, played a live pre-show on the plaza. They hit the goal to captivate people who had not been to the Rock Hall, as Cathryn jokes, "I'd never seen that many 11-year-old girls here in my life."

The Rock Hall is "adding to the authentic experience of going to a concert, but also providing [people] with something that's on the way through that we can benefit from," Zoe points out. Taylgate hits on the Rock Hall's other benchmarks to connect with community, connect with their preexisting partners like Kiss FM, and to add extra value to Taylor Swift fans' experience. It's a win-win.

Rock Hall asks, "How can you get people engaged in music in an educational and productive way, not just listening for the sake of listening?" and they answer in the way they design their program. It's through Women Who Rock, Rock and Recovery, Klipschfest, and Taylgate that guests can connect in a purposeful way with the music.

Guests learn about the music and story behind it through the number of activities on site. Learning does not have to come in the form of serious, tangible knowledge you read on the museum walls next to the artifacts. Learning happens through experience.

At Rock Hall music is placed more purposefully than trans-actionally. Music's purpose can be meditation, encouragement of dance and movement, stimulation of creativity, or connection with people of similar interests. With Rock Hall's clear understanding of the mission to connect the past and present, they tie a greater purpose to the way visitors experience music in the present, which then shapes the future.

Ingredients

Deep understanding of one's mission.

Rock Hall's mission is "to engage, teach and inspire through the power of rock and roll."[35] Everything ties back to this goal to connect the past and the present. There are people like Zoe, whose job is to see that the mission at the center of every department's work and focus.

Simon Sinek codified how powerful leaders are able to inspire others with how they think, act and communicate. He calls his code the "golden circle" and defines his theory in his TED Talk called "How great leaders inspire action."[36] The pattern asks three questions: Why? How? What?

- Why? – Why do you do it? Why do you get out of bed and do what you do every day?
- How? – How do you do it? What is the value proposition?
- What? – What do you do?

Every organization knows what they do and that is often what they lead with in pitching themselves to customers. Yet, inspired leaders lead with their why, their purpose. Take Apple for example. They could say:

- What? – We make great computers.
- How? – They are beautifully designed, simple to use and user-friendly.
- Why? – Want to buy one?

That is not the way Apple does it. They follow the "golden circle" from the inside out saying:

- Why? – "In everything we do, we believe in challenging the status quo. We believe in thinking differently."
- How? – "The way we challenge the status quo is by making our computers beautifully designed, simple to use and user-friendly."
- What? – "Want to buy one?"[37]

The same approach is used at The Rock Hall:

- Why? Everything we do connects the past to the present and inspires the future of rock and roll.
- How? The way we inspire is through programming and exhibits that engage and teach through rock and roll.
- What? Want to come visit us?

The Rock Hall knows their why and they live it out.

Collaboration.

This is how Women Who Rock succeeded, Rock and Recovery was born, and Klipschfest became an annual event.

Rock Hall can create energy in Cleveland as can any organization in the city. However, it is in aligning forces and collaborating that real momentum and energy is sparked.

It is both internal collaboration that creates a well rounded, interactive, and educational experience along with external collaboration that allows Rock Hall, a nonprofit, to obtain the resources and opportunity to maximize their potential. It is collaboration that creates a space for the community to come and celebrate on birthdays and death anniversaries of Rock Hall inductees. In 2016 on what would have been Prince's 58th birthday, Rock Hall hosted a free celebration of his life. There was a Prince cover band, special exhibit, costume contest, trivia, and streaming of Prince's Induction Ceremony performance. They all came together in the spirit of collaboration.

CHAPTER 11

LIVE MUSIC IS AN OASIS

———

"Let's do a concert on a boat," Andy Levine, the founder of Sixthman, said back in 2001. At the time, Andy was managing Sister Hazel, an alternative rock band, out of Gainesville, Florida. He figured setting sail from Tampa to Key West, Florida to Cozumel, Mexico with the band's fans would be a fun, new way to experience the music. They coined this extravaganza Rock Boat.

Rock Boat continued to cruise along the Gulf of Mexico annually until Sixthman, the company Andy founded to oversee this travel musical spectacular, hit a rock in a hard place when Hurricane Katrina struck in 2005. Rock Boat was cancelled and it seemed like an unpleasant date with destiny for Sixthman. But fans came back saying, "keep our money... just don't go out of business."

A call from the Barenaked Ladies at the end of December 2005, paired with the dedication of Sixthman alumni cruisers, gave Andy the energy he needed to move into the new year. The Barenaked Ladies' manager asked if Andy could help put on a cruise for the band and their fans. Andy responded "We've been waiting on your call."

They built out the experience that surrounded the cruise, adding a curated lineup before the main act. Top-tier names started jumping on board, like John Mayer, Kid Rock, and Zac Brown Band. Andy quickly realized this was not just a concert on a boat, but that it could be "a music festival on a ship."

In 2011 Anthony Diaz joined the Sixthman team as the Chief Marketing Officer. He really looked at who Sixthman was and what they were doing. As it was offering 12 cruises that year featuring full lineups, Anthony realized that this was "not just a music festival, [it was a] vacation."

Expectations for vacation look a lot different than expectations that one may have when going to a concert. If you go to a concert tonight at your local House of Blues or favorite neighborhood venue, as long as the wine is good or there is cold beer on tap, the room temperature is comfortable, people are nice, there is parking and security and the performance is solid – it is a good experience. When you plan all year for a vacation and pay a premium price for a premium experience, the expectations of service change drastically. Anthony, who now serves as Sixthman's CEO, remarked, "We are probably competing more in your vacation decision, not your music decision."

Think about the last time you went on vacation. Maybe you went with your boyfriend or girlfriend? Your family? Extended family? A group of friends? Or maybe you went on your own? Imagine the last place you went to whether it be the Grand Canyon or Paris or some little beach town.

Envision that place.

Imagine you are walking around that place and everyone is a friend or family member. You are in this new place, but somehow you are connected to everyone you meet. That is what a Sixthman cruise feels like.

When people board the Sixthman ship for Rock Boat with Sister Hazel or Ke$ha's Weird & Wonderful Rainbow Ride or Runaway to Paradise with Jon Bon Jovi, they have a connection with the artist and therefore will connect with all the other people on the boat more quickly due to their shared interest.

Anthony goes on to explain that on a Sixthman cruise, "you're around people who share a similar passion. What's cool about that is it's a passion. It is not like they're just like you. They're really diverse crowds."

That's how Anthony got hooked. He went on the second annual Rock Boat back in 2002 when Andy, his buddy from college at the University of Florida, coerced him into trying out this new, exciting music experience model he had created for Sister Hazel fans. Anthony and Andy played in a band, Water Dog, in college. Anthony played drums and marketed the band while Andy was busy booking the shows when he was not playing guitar on stage.

The band's talent on stage was no match for the magic they worked behind the scenes.

Early on Anthony and Andy saw great value in treating everyone nicely, as simple as it sounds. They brought gifts to venues, wrote thank-you notes to the guys they rented equipment from and wrote fan mail to their own fans. Anthony jokes, "Our best way of grueling was just to super serve everyone in the ecosystem. Maybe because we just weren't that good of a band meant we had to be good at something else."

They mastered the art of hospitality towards those who were suppose to host them. This same dedication to everyone in the ecosystem can be seen in the way the team at Sixthman operates today under the motto "LIVE LOUD."

Unfortunately, their craftsmanship and networking behind the scenes could only get them so far. Water Dog needed a record deal if they were going to survive after college. Spotify and YouTube did not exist to give Water Dog the flexibility to pursue a full-time career in music.

The band split up.

Anthony, looking at his degree in journalism and his journey with music over the last few years, figured, "I'm going to go work at a radio station. It's music, but it's business."

Andy figured he would put the guitar to rest and dive into what he was really good at, managing. The rest of the band joined up with a group in Gainesville, Florida that was gaining traction, Sister Hazel, and Andy served as their manager.

Anthony admits that when he first experienced Sixthman's Rock Boat in 2002, "I was really impressed by the whole idea."

In the comfort of his media job, Anthony stayed put and kept in touch with Andy. They collaborated with one another as they grew in their respective businesses talking about balancing life at home with their wives and kids. In 2011, when Andy was really trying to grow the company he asked Anthony, "What do you think about joining me in this venture and seeing if we can grow the company?"

Anthony took the gamble. He was drawn to the notion of serving fans as they had when they were part of Water Dog. He was excited when he considered how they could really change people's feelings and improve their year if they could give them a memorable vacation experience.

With this curiosity and drive, Anthony has advanced from Chief Marketing Officer to Chief Operations Officer to his current role as Chief Executive Officer. During his eight years at Sixthman a lot has happened. The company has grown from 20 employees to over 65, will be running 18 cruises in 2019, are breaking into new markets internationally with three shows sailing out of Barcelona in 2019, are entering the resort festival scene, as well as expanding to sports and comedy entertainment.

"While the live music industry—and music business overall—has radically changed since Sixthman first set sail, our focus to tear down the walls between fans and bands and create a truly special guest experience from ship to shore has never changed and remains our compass in all decisions we make to this day," Anthony says.

Artists are multidimensional, not just touring musicians. Anthony points out that an artist "might have a book, they might be in a movie, they might have a perfume, they might have a clothing line, they might have a charity, a foundation. We can bring all of that to life at sea. By doing so we're immersing the fans in the entire world of the artist which is really compelling for the guest."

Question and answers sessions, stripped down sets, light-hearted games of Family Feud hosted by artists, and collaborative lineups are just a few of the layers of engagement that fans can only get, or really have time for, at a resort or on a cruise ship.

There is no division between the artists and fans. Paramore, the pop rock band from Franklin, Tennessee has a signature cruise that sold out in pre-sale to 2,700 fans before the full lineup was announced in 2018. There was pure excitement around the young, edgy band that drew this dedicated crowd.

At 5 p.m. on April 6th, 2018 the Norwegian Pearl set off from Miami in sight of the Bahamas. Indie rock vibes filled the air as MewithoutYou kicked off the day. Paramore played their first set of the weekend at 8 p.m. as night fell. They capped the night off center stage with their most recent single, "Rose Colored Boy," with a mini-cover of "I Wanna Dance With Somebody" mixed into the final chorus.

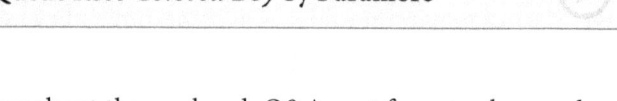

Queue *Rose Colored Boy* by Paramore

Throughout the weekend, Q&As got fans up close and personal with both the goofy side and heart-wrenching realities of vocalist Hayley Williams, guitarist Taylor York and drummer Zac Farro offstage. Fans experienced Paramore's set opening with a cover of Drake's "Passionfruit." Fans had the chance to perform for Paramore as the band judged "Paraoke," the third annual karaoke contest. Fans also had the chance to discover artists throughout the cruise that Sixthman had identified as artists akin to Paramore. Local Natives, Judah & the Lion, Halfnoise, MewithoutYou, Now, Now, and Mija are among the bands that glided across the Atlantic for four days with Paramore and its fans.

Brian Macdonald, the mandolin player and back vocalist of Judah and the Lion, shared about the Parahoy! voyage, "It feels like camp, where you run into a lot of the same people, with a lot of positive energy and high-fives."[38]

High fives all around tear down the walls between Paramore and the fans. Ship dwellers are given the opportunity to

"LIVE LOUD." Sixthman makes sure their guests, partners, and their team feel like the stars. This exceptional level of hospitality can be traced back to the days of Water Dog when Anthony and Andy thanked everyone who laid eyes on them in a thoughtful, personal way. Conceptualized from a "concert on a boat" to a "festival on a ship" to a "vacation," Sixthman has designed a whimsical oasis for music lovers to come together as a community to support their favorite artists.

Ingredients

Super serve the ecosystem

Everyone is a star. Guests, partners, artists and team members are each served with passion on a Sixthman cruise. To super serve the ecosystem you are in, you don't have to go as far as gifting every venue or writing thank-you notes for everyone you encounter. It can be simpler than that— a memento that speaks to the experience. It could be a sticker – something that fans can rep that serves as a conversation point when someone notices it. It could be a card—a hip business card if you will. This card communicates who you are and what you stand for, a sort of manifesto. Personalize it. Brett Newski (you met him in Chapter 6) has the best business cards. He has an illustration of him on the front with a speech bubble. When I met him he looked me straight in the eyes, asked me my name, and wrote "hi Katie" in the bubble and handed it to me with his information on the back. It could be even simpler. Being nice would fulfill the simple call to action Anthony and Andy took during their Water Dog days. Being nice served their ecosystem and them quite well.

No walls on an oasis

It is a friendship and exchange both in music, art, and conversation. Q&A, games and simply vacationing together means bands and fans are one unit, one community. You can have a concert anywhere but the mindset changes when you set sail away from land and the responsibilities rooted on home soil. Since not everyone has the luxury of setting sail for a few days, how can this mentality— sailing into a new reality— be recreated on land? The answer is no walls. Through mixing the media of music, art, storytelling, and games, layers of character and personality are unpacked in which fans can immerse themselves.

CHAPTER 12

LIVE MUSIC IS A FEST

Bonnaroo is Creole slang for "good stuff."

Kerry Black, Rick Farman, Richard Goodstone, and Jonathan Mayers went to college together in New Orleans. Inspired by R&B singer Dr. John's 1974 album "Desitively Bonnaroo" they choose the name to honor the rich Louisiana music history. The recent college grads looked to turn their passion for music into a career. They dreamt up a festival to take place in Manchester, Tennessee that pulled in elements from festivals they attended in the 90s, like Phish's festival. They paired up with Ashley Capps of AC Entertainment to host Bonnaroo in 2002. Tickets went on sale for the inaugural festival and two weeks later were sold out.

Bonnaroo was named by Rolling Stone as one of "50 Moments that Changed the History of Rock & Roll". This four-day celebration of music has become a cornerstone of American Music Festivals, taking place annually on 700 acres at Great Stage Park coined "The Farm." Fans have claimed Bonnaroo to be "a rite of passage experience," with over 120 musical acts, 16 stages, a massive water slide, and pop-up experiences around every corner.

Superfly, the live entertainment and marketing company that co-founded Bonnaroo, works around a common purpose to create "shared experiences that enrich lives and unite communities." Chris Sampson, EVP of Programming at Superfly, overseas talent booking and programming for Bonnaroo, Outside Lands and Clusterfest. Each festival is unique year to year, with different people partaking to make up the festival community for a few days. Chris explains, "it's not just like a neighborhood where the same 10 or 12 houses live there and it's the same kind of families. You have a situation where you have 20,000 to 30,000 people for some of the smaller festivals to 70,000 or 80,000 people for some of the bigger festivals and so every year, every festival takes on a different look and feel."

What particularly strikes Chris is watching the impact that the festival community has on the artists. "You see an artist take the stage at Bonnaroo and a few songs into his or her set, they kind of look out over the vast sea of people and you can see them literally take it in, breathe in the air of the audience and the community can feel that energy," he says.

This dynamic between the audience and the artist makes the festival.

Chris further explains, "a lot of people who go to Bonnaroo are looking to escape for four days and be turned onto new music and meet new people and I think the artists who are on stage really feel that and they experience it as well."

As people greet one another with high fives and smiles as they enter and exit the festival grounds, Bonnaroovians clearly embody the spirit of meeting new people. Infected by positivity, festival goers are said to be open and excited about exploring new sounds. Fans adopt this energy and as Chris shared, so do the bands.

My Morning Jacket, one of Chris's favorite bands, played the second stage at Bonnaroo in 2008. Like all great summer Tennessee days there was a chance of thunderstorms. The sky turned green and the air was hot, fans waited for the heavens to open and rain to start pouring down. "The band went with it," Chris recalls, "and you could feel the music, their energy and pace change as the weather changed. It was this incredible moment where the audience and the artist and the weather all were one."

An element that no one could have predicted or planned for became a special moment for Bonnaroovians and My Morning Jacket. Chris describes it as a "guitar solo from the sky," that energized and electrified the fans and the band.

In the past few years, critics have not looked at the festival with the same googly eyes as many returning fans and event organizers like Chris. Well regarded music critics of *The New York Times*, Jon Pareles, Ben Ratliff, and Jon Caramanica, wrote "Why We're Not Making Plans for Coachella and Bonnaroo" in March of 2016. When the new year hits, festival lineups start coming out. As they trickle in, the trio of music fanatics have become reluctant to put their hands up to attend the festivals saying, "we delay putting our hands up because we are trying to figure out intelligent ways to cover the big, cross-genre, medium-cool outdoor pop festivals, which look increasingly alike in their vision of a codified, consensual, safe and purchasable bohemia." [39]

Their biggest complaint – the music. They go as far as to say, "their bookings used to be somewhat exciting, if exciting means special and special means rare and rare means meaningful; they aren't anymore."[40]

The critics argue lineups at different festivals are not all that different. Counterparts argue the fest is not about the music, it is about the experience. So, a *music* festival is not about music? For the music critics whose expertise is in music, that is a tough pill to swallow. Chris acknowledges this problem they often run into when their lineup at Bonnaroo does look similar to other major music festivals. That is why they differentiate themselves with the non-music experiences they offer on-site – – the food, drink, activities, and activations. With any festival, there is a subculture that sets the vibe and draws the crowd. It's the fashion and the regional environment that promoters can inadvertently sell. A great escape and immersion into happiness on The Farm is what Bonnaroo is selling just as much if not more than headliners like Eminem, the Killers, and Muse in 2018.

With the current state of festivals, Jon Pareles, chief popular music critic at *The New York Times*, asks, "Where might one go, then, to learn more about music as it's currently being made and played in this country?"[41]

His instinct is to go to smaller festivals and music gatherings. Jon's thought process is that "Readers get a better deal when we take them to a festival that has a story in it: a story about an aesthetic, a region, a reaction, maybe even a cool clique."

The point seems to be that major festival like Bonnaroo started with this character representative of the region, the community, or the environment but as they have grown, they lost the scrappy, authentic character in their roots. In 2016, when the critique article was written, Bonnaroo took a rough hit with a reported low attendance of 45,000.[42] However, in the past two years, they have been able to bring attendance backup in. With time, the crowd has seemingly got younger and younger. Catering to this audience may attribute to the shift from rock and jam band headliners closing out the weekend to pop stars like The Weeknd in 2017.

Well, there is truth to what the three men at *The New York Times* offered, that is the opinion of three critics. Bonnaroo brings upwards of 100,000 people to Manchester, Tennessee annually. Clearly, they are doing something right whether it be about the music or the experience. Bonnaroo and major music festivals, in general, are experiments in ephemeral, temporary community. They are fans sweet escape.

Ingredients

Enhance the Non-Music Experience

The regional environment and pop-up experiences. Embrace them and give them a place on the stage.

That is the business of Jack Shannon, CEO, and Co-Found of RECESS. RECESS pairs universities with brands so they can make money on their events and create engaging experiences on college campuses during festivals and concerts. Sure, in many ways it is a marketing ploy but experiential marketing is this growing trend that resonates with millennials and Gen Z. Jack has set up a number of activations with Red Bull on college campuses. Red Bull caps off their activations with a chance for a lucky student to go to their headquarters. "We are pushing brands to provide authentic value," Shannon says. Red Bull provides a once in a lifetime experience, that is authentic value.

In the music festival scene, beyond college campuses, brands can add authentic value in this same way. As a brand, they can be the drink that quenches fans thirst in between sets, the branded poncho the crowd wears when the weather takes a tole, or the prize that people can enter to win creating a buzz. We have seen it all done before.

But, pop-up activations do not need to be purely marketing based. Pop-ups come in many forms from art activations to advocacy work. These pop-ups offer a space to tell a rich story about the region which critics and fans alike crave. So what if every festival or musical event leaned into the local culture? All food and merch locally sourced. Cultural immersion with story activations in forms of art beyond the music – painting, murals, dancing, writing, and the list goes on. This is yet another medium that gives fans the opportunity to escape for a few days into a different physical and mental space. This adds true authentic value.

PART 2

LIVE MUSIC: INGREDIENTS FROM BEYOND

If you are looking to disrupt an industry, you don't turn to your peers to see what they are doing, you look beyond your present circumstances. Jen Hyman looked at the digital cloud and asked, "Why can't we do that with clothes?" Thus, Rent the Runway, an online closet of designer dresses and accessories available for rent, was born. Jen used concepts from the technology industry to disrupt the trillion-dollar fashion industry.

What elements can we steal from outside the music entertainment industry to incorporate and enhance what is happening within the live music experience?

In this section, some gifted creators of community:

- Pack up for adult, digital detox camp
- Practice their best downward dog
- Make pasta in a stranger's kitchen
- Befriend members of the Krishna cult.

In seemingly unrelated settings, these adventures offer keys to cultivating community and creating an environment for engaging experiences. With a little distance from the music scene, these communities trigger novel ideas and offer possibilities for innovation in the live music experience.

These adventures offer ingredients for creating an event and space where guests can Live LIVE! in a new music experience. Here, the ingredients that emerge have everything to do with culture, from creating a manifesto to practicing ABCD ("always be connecting dots"). Watch as insight emerges from everyday happenings as well as from outlandish events, offering a new way to look at and create live music experiences.

You ready for this adventure? It's your time to Live LIVE!

CHAPTER 13

LIVE MUSIC IS
A RETREAT

———

If you follow Otto Road into the mountain holler outside of Spencer, West Virginia, you'll find Jeannie Kirkhope and her partner Bill living a simple life in the Appalachian Mountains. While they live the life of hermits with their dogs, chickens, and goats, living in a remote location, Jeannie has her finger on the pulse of some of the deepest systemic issues in the region and the world. She works tirelessly as an advocate for change, running the Appalachia Catholic Worker Farm with the mission "to provide spiritual space and hope in the mountains by addressing issues of poverty, in the context of all creation, through Education, Contemplation and Outreach."

Community, being the people we are surrounded by every day, is always present and at the center of Jeannie's work. She believes that "somewhere deep inside of us we know we all rely on each other."

There is interdependence and interconnectedness we rely on for the benefit of everyone. Jeannie has dedicated her life to living in community and solidarity with the people of Appalachia, as well as to bringing in new communities to the space to educate them on the Appalachian Region's land, culture, religion, social issues, environmental issues, and political dilemmas.

"Part of the definition of community is including your environment, whether it is land or dedication and commitment to the space." This dedication to the land looks different in varying landscapes.

"Resourcefulness in what you have around you is part of community," Jeannie says as she reflects on work she has done with homeless people in the U.S. An urban-centered downtown is where homeless people go in many cities. As if it were a literal home, these men and women will call to friends across the street as if they were across the hall. These people learn to be resourceful in the environment, finding shelter, food, and care for their basic needs in their immediate surroundings. It is this resourcefulness that brings them closer to the land and closer to one another.

Jeannie points out how important it is in a rural or urban space to connect with the environment on a conscious level. Different from those experiencing homelessness in an urban center, the rural Appalachian community is connected to their environment through familial generations that have come and gone, as well as through caring for the land and its inhabitants. "There is so much knowledge to be had over one's lifetime. Top [that with] generations in the same place and you just become one with your place," Jeannie says when thinking about Appalachian people's connection to their environment. The Appalachian people do not leave the region or even their own holler range because it is so familiar and a defining factor of their identity.

Mainstream society is mobile given our ultra-connected lifestyle. People go to college in a different town than they grew up in, they get a job in yet another city, and are able to pivot with ease. There is no longer such a strong connection to the land.

It is different then for generations past, which is okay.

Jeannie too was mobile in that way. She grew up in Toledo, Ohio, went to school in Cleveland and then lived in Seattle,

Washington. Once in Appalachia she felt at home. She had the strongest connection to the environment and its makeup so she put her roots down.

She tells others that "once you find a home, put down roots and put the world around you like a little turtle shell." Jeannie giggles.

In her little school house, Jeannie hosts groups of students to learn about the Appalachian region and grow in self-knowledge so they too can get closer to their home and begin to lay their roots. She creates community from scratch each time a new group comes through the doors of her humble home for a retreat or mission trip. Looking at the Maslow Hierarchy of needs, a psychology theory based on humans' innate curiosity, she starts with the basics.

The foundational level consists of basic needs including food, water, warmth, and rest. Upon arrival, Jeannie makes sure the group knows where the bathroom is and shows them where they are going to sleep. In doing so, Jeannie shows that she is offering a safe, comfortable, and warm space, factors people may be subconsciously be worried about. Groups travel far and wide to make it to Jeannie's neck of the woods, so she offers food and drink as they walk in the door.

From there, she works her way up the hierarchy to the needs for belonging, esteem, and self – actualization.

Rituals are a tactic that Jeannie uses to create a sense of belonging. At the end of the day's activities, Jeannie invites retreat attendees to a reflection ritual. Sitting in a circle, the group surrounds a large candle that Jeannie lovingly calls "the God candle." Jeannie poses a question to the group and each participant answers on their own time as they simultaneously light a smaller candle from "the God candle" and hold onto it. Participants have the platform to share their own thoughts. While opinions and thoughts are diverse, "there is something we all share in common," Jeannie says. Everyone completes the same action, lighting their candle in a common space.

Jeannie is a social justice warrior for sure – she has sparked change in the Appalachian region and pushed policy reform for mountaintop removal, LGBTQ rights, and other social and environmental issues. She had a gift, offering a special energy in these small group settings, sparking interpersonal and intrinsic change in the people and communities she forms on these retreats and mission trips. It is through her sense of place and use of the Maslow Hierarchy of Needs that she inspires people to be more purposeful in their activities, communities, and environments.

Ingredients

A rooted place

This one is a little puzzling for touring musicians who make their livelihood on touring and traveling. But there is something to be said about knowing your roots and sticking with them. Rex Larkman, the drummer for the Cleveland born and bred, reggae, funk band Tropidelic, has toured the U.S. coast to coast. When asked about his dream show he envisions playing Jacob's Pavilion with the Cuyahoga River and Cleveland skyline as the backdrop on a summer night with all his hometown family, friends, and fans selling out the crowd. What if fans traveled for bands instead of the other way around? Would bands like Tropidelic be more authentic? Maybe it is too radical, but what if artists brought a piece of home with them? Chance the Rapper is branded as a Chicagoan, and proud of it. When Chance plays a show in Austin or Boston or Los Angeles, he brings a piece of Chicago with him. It is a huge part of his character and his music. What if more artists integrated the story of their roots into their performance in a deliberate way?

Space and ritual

Jeannie uses a candle to bring different people and opinions together in a shared physical act. Ritual is a way to bring purpose and reflection to routine. You hear a lot about pre-show rituals in live music – Foo Fighters take shots of Jägermeister as they dance to Michael Jackson, John Legend eats half of a rotisserie chicken, and Queen B, Miss Beyoncé, says a prayer and stretches with her entourage. Let's bring more of that to the stage and invite fans to be part of these rituals. Maggie Rogers plays "I Wanna Dance with Somebody" by Whitney Houston at the end of every concert.

> **Queue *I Wanna Dance With Somebody* by Whitney Houston**

Each show ends as a Whitney Houston big dance party and celebration of joy. While she has never come out and said why she plays this song at the end of each show, Maggie has shared how dancing has been transformative in her career and personal growth. When talking about how she creates her music with *The Guardian*, she said, "You need music that is compelling and intellectual, but you also need music that just feels good and you can laugh about and dance to, and I think I'm trying to marry the two in some way."[43] Maggie, a true dancing queen, has used the power of dance to bring people together. Fans have tweeted and had conversations on social media sharing how this ritual has left them feeling happier, saying "the world needs more of this."

CHAPTER 14

LIVE MUSIC IS IN DOWNWARD DOG

"We crave connection with other humans. We feed off of each other's energy. That kind of environment — where you all come together and there's a common intention — it's really powerful," says Tammy Lyons. For Tammy, yoga is a space that she gathers with people of common intent.

Tammy first came to the mat and practiced yoga in 2000. It was then that she fell in love with deliberate physical motion and harnessing breath in the practice. Since then she has opened three studios called Inner Bliss Yoga Studios in the Cleveland area. Additionally Tammy and the Inner Bliss teams serve as the official yoga provider for the Cleveland Indians baseball team and teach over 2,200 students a week in their studios.

In the summer of 2013, Tammy worked with a group of co-founders to dream up an event that would celebrate the city of Cleveland, a city that many have doubted. She used movement and breath to turn doubt into celebration. They coined this event, Believe in CLE.

Inner Bliss collaborated with the local Lululemon Athletica to put on Believe in CLE, a free night of yoga at the Rock and Roll Hall of Fame plaza. The Cleveland skyline was the backdrop as good vibrations ran through 1,400 yogis, setting the record for the largest outdoor yoga event in Cleveland history.

The tradition continues into 2018, on a crisp Friday night in August. Tammy leads the 2,400 yogis, kicking off the practice with an invitation to share a hug and meet a neighbor. Tammy's practice is unlike most. Dance parties break out in between downward dogs as yogis link arms and run in circles like they are at a barn dance, wind in their hair and happy smiles on their faces. In warrior one position, neighbors grab hands and lift one another up towards the sky.

The mass of people flows through a cycle of vinyasas as Bruce Springsteen booms through the speakers.

Queue *Born In The U.S.A.* by Bruce Springsteen

Tammy sees a little boy out of the corner of her eye running around on top of the elevated ornamentation at the center of the plaza that yogis surround. The boy makes a fuss, "I don't want to be here," he yells at his dad who lays, unfazed, in savasana.

Tammy approaches the little boy, gets on his level, looks him directly in the eye and says, "Do you want a hug?"

The boy's eyes light up as he proclaims, "yes," and she embraces him.

He whispers in her ear, "He promised me ice cream," and continues to babble as Tammy brings him in closer.

The tighter she squeezes, the quieter and calmer the boy gets. Deep in practice, only one person in the crowd saw this encounter and was moved by the simple beauty of the transformation of emotions in the boy's face because Tammy got on his level and offered him her attention. Tammy proved her own point: "We crave connection with other humans." Sure, this little boy wanted ice cream, but more than anything he just wanted someone to notice him.

Ingredients

Prescribed movement

Those stupid smiles that yogis had on their face as they did a "Cotton Eye Joe" type of jig were orchestrated by Tammy's dance instructions. Dancing is a very vulnerable act; people do not want to make fools out of themselves so they often shy away from moving and grooving. But Tammy offered simple instructions for everyone to dance together, not just side by side but physically together. Dance moves had a way of physically connecting the crowd, whether it was through linking arms or holding hands. So, if one person made a fool out of themselves, so did everyone. Artists instruct people to clap their hands, raise their hands, and jump, but what if they invited fans to hold hands and lift one another up? Would the physical connection create a stronger bond among the whole audience? Maybe it would just be awkward? Zumba, a Latin dance-inspired workout, is reportedly performed by more than 15 million people at 200,000 locations in 180 countries around the world. Zumba is prescribed movement.[44] A study reported in *TIME* magazine found that women who did Zumba for just eight weeks saw their quality of life scores jump by 9% and their self-esteem increase by 16%.[45] These women by no means were dancing experts but they just started swinging their hips as they followed the instructor. Could more purposeful pre-scribed movement in live music experiences offer the same?

CHAPTER 15

LIVE MUSIC IS CAMP

In a yellow school bus, campers ages 20+ ride north for four hours from the hilltop of Mission Dolores Park hugged by the San Francisco skyline off to a small seaside town in Mendocino, California. "Prepare to step off the grid," the sign reads as campers roll up to this alternative universe.

There are a few rules at camp. There are no bedtimes mandated for these adults, but instead no phones, no computers, no digital technology, no booze or drugs, no talk of age, and absolutely no talk of work are allowed on the premises.

Email inboxes are replaced with old school mailboxes that campers fill with hand-written notes and trinkets they create.

Google is replaced by the "Human Powered Search Engine," a wall with campers' pressing questions scribbled on scratch paper that community members respond to. Keyboards and touch screens are replaced by typewriters that remind campers that some writing is best left unedited, whatever you put out is part of the creative process.

"People do not have the chance to say 'what am I' if I'm not what I do,"[46] founder Levi Felix remarked, reflecting on how we are all our own personal brands and tiny corporations as our digital identities created via social media define our real life interactions. Adult identity has become defined by work. Levi designed Camp Grounded to be a place where campers create an alter-ego, their nickname for the weekend, and are recognized for who they are in the present moment. For some that means they are king of Capture the Flag while someone is a talented artist. People can find their niche somewhere in over fifty activities over the three-day weekend getaway.

Jillian Richards, an author and community builder who currently resides in New York, traded in her life in the Big Apple for a weekend to detox and get weird with a group of strangers in California. "It opened my eyes to what is possible in community," she says. "I got closer with people in those three days than people I have known for years."

Jillian realized just how different this experience would be when they pulled up to camp on the yellow school bus and their bus leader, a Camp Grounded staff member, explained what camp meant to her.

On the leader's first ride up to camp she sat with a pad of paper in her lap and drew what was happening around her. She passed it around and turned it into a little game. Riders around her added to the picture. They pulled up to camp and unloaded. She turned to a camp worker she had just met and asked him, "Want to play?"

Suddenly she was elevated off the ground and being spun by this man she had just met as he proclaimed, "You get it! You belong here!" As a new camper, she understood that the top priority at camp was to play and she, with her energy and ideas, had already brought something unique into the Camp Grounded community.

Now serving as a Camp Grounded staff member, she recalls this story and gets teary-eyed as she welcomes Jillian and the rest of the crew into camp. A field lays before Jillian, hugs and high fives awaiting, as thirty camp counselors blow bubbles and play music. "I had never felt so welcomed into a space so immediately," Jillian recalls. "I felt so cared for before it even started at all, these people made this for me."

For three days Jillian was immersed in this happy-go-lucky, yet vulnerable and intentional world. But once it is over, the question is, where do you go from here?

Jillian distinctly remembers thinking, "This is great, it was an awesome weekend but this is just going to be another one of those times where you had a great weekend and you say you are going to talk to these people but then you never talk to them again and life goes back to being exactly the same."

However, Jillian found this wasn't the case. The fellow New Yorkers she met that weekend wanted to take the culture of Camp Grounded back to their home base and spend time with each other constantly. Jillian says, "We all wanted to bring it into our lives and that was something I hadn't experienced before."

They met up at a bar a week after camp. While they were now breaking the camp's no booze rule, they honored the rule of no phones. They shut down their devices, threw them in a basket, and forgot about them for the evening. They channeled their ultra-ego and played games, inviting their new barstool buddies to play with them.

Jillian recalls the day as if it were yesterday, saying, "We were being these total weirdos at this outdoor bar just asking to paint strangers' faces and trying to get the whole bar to do the wave with us. It was this culture of playfulness that we had through the weekend; we actually brought [it] back to our lives. I realize how rare that is and it only happened because the culture of that event is so strong and meant so much to all of us."

That is what Levi envisioned back home— a movement of play, mindfulness, and connectivity where people "use their devices and screens to stay in contact but organize in public spaces to celebrate life."[47] Levy left a powerful legacy of intentional living when he passed at the young age of 32 in 2017.

Jillian has gone above and beyond in bringing the Camp Grounded culture back to New York. She is not just hanging out with past campers, she is connecting more New Yorkers to the celebration of life with purpose. The Joy List, a weekly newsletter, is her brainchild and a resource for people to find events that "they can go to by themselves, and leave with a new friend. It's a way to highlight the amazing work that people in this city are doing to spread positivity and connectedness. And it's a weekly gratitude practice for us, to remember that NYC is filled with love-- even though it doesn't feel like that sometimes."

Events have the power to "introduce you to people that can completely change your life," Jillian says. That is what Camp Grounded did for her, it changed her life. Now, she is changing New Yorkers' lives and lifestyles to be more intentional and fulfilling.

Ingredients

Celebrating Life in Public Spaces

The celebratory tone is set at Camp Grounded with the rules laid out before the group even meets. If you open an event to anyone, then you get random people and unclear expectations. However, with rules and clear expectations, the right people end up in the room; they know why they are there and what they have in common with other event goers. What if concerts were labeled by their intention? John Mayer was one of the artists, along with Lady Gaga and Post Malone, who participated in Bud Light's Dive Bar series. On a warm night in June 2017, Mayer played with a full band at Echoplex in Los Angeles, a 500-capacity venue. No phones were allowed as Mayer shredded alongside Alessia Cara. They closed the set with his 2005 hit "Gravity."[48]

Queue *Gravity* by John Mayer

Sure, there was a professional camera crew catching the action for Facebook live streamers as fans in person enjoyed the music and a cold one on Bud Light. Those in the crowd were challenged to be present and experience the moment without their personal devices. "This is one of those things where it shakes you out of the loop. I get to play in a little club and have fun," Mayer said from the stage. "This is an outlier. I enjoy it very much."[49] The rules do not have to be as strict as "no phones" for a music experience to shake a crowd out of the normal loop into something different and exciting. Since John Mayer has an extensive roster of songs that cover a range of emotions over his seven studio albums, we will continue using him as an example. Maybe Mayer has a set that he could curate with songs meant for dancing— real dancing, not just bopping your head. So you call that "John Mayer's Dance Show" and people show up with the expectation that they will grab their neighbor's hand and be shaking your hips. Perhaps he wants to play a set that will be savored and sing lyrics that will be listened to. We could call that "John Mayer Acoustic," put Mayer on the stage with a stoop and an acoustic guitar, and tell fans to show up with the intention to sit to listen intently.

The list goes on – there could be the "John Mayer's Greatest Hit Show" with songs all the fans want to hear or "hidden gems," the songs the Mayer holds near and dear but maybe flew past fans' radars. Sure, we label bands by genre and that comes with a perceived notion of the energy around the music experience. But, by labeling shows, fans can choose the shows that are their speed when expectations that come with genres are not clear. This could aid in music discovery. It's like *Choose Your Own Adventure* books. Lesser-known artists categorized by this system could attract fans that enjoy music experiences centered around dance, simply listening, meeting other fans, light shows, theatrical presentation, or another category.

CHAPTER 16

LIVE MUSIC IS A PERSONALIZED TOUR FOR TOURISTS

Luis Pincay has traveled the globe. He backpacked through South America with a group and led tours through some of the most spectacular scenes in the world. He traveled over 50,000 nautical miles with the U.S. Coast Guard as a Petty officer second class, working as a food service specialist serving 140+ people daily. He has been with Airbnb for over five years now but still travels quite often as the General Manager of Mexico and Central America Experiences. His job is to connect people who have a love for cooking, photography, knitting, yoga, or horseback riding, to someone who wants to learn about their passion.

Luis has a finger on the pulse of what hospitality looks and feels like at its best. "People offer you whatever they [have] and they made you part of their household right away," Luis points out when reflecting on his time backpacking through rural South America. When he was brought on the experienced team at Airbnb, he wanted to help hosts learn from one another and lift one another up, emulating his experience in his travels and his own family life.

Experiences are a feature the Airbnb platform launched in 2016, allowing tourists to live like locals. Experiences have been so successful because they are built on passion. Having this passion, a strong belief and motivation in one's work, is a major key to success in business. Some of the most prominent businesses, such as Apple, Nike, and yes, Airbnb, are successful because of their founders' passion for what they do. In addition, their passion comes across in effective communication of their why, the root of their passion, which then draws in customers. Experience hosts share their passion and, as Luis says, "They are more willing to share who they are as a person as well. Because it's part of who they are, the other person (the customer or guest) [who] is trying to learn is more willing to learn and understand."

Luis jokes about how the idea sound romantic but in reality, passion "creates a friendship."

Chillies with an Expert is an experience that sticks out to Luis and happens to be a favorite of 150 others who have reviewed the experience and given it five stars on Airbnb's website. Fernando is the experience host, the grandson of one of the main chili traders in Mexico City and with his family owns "La Flor de Jamaica." He created the first gastronomic workshop in Mexico focused on spreading knowledge of a main national ingredient, the chili pepper. Through his eyes, he tells Luis and guests stories of his life and his family's as they walk through the Jamaica Market, meet Fernando's market friends and learn about their unique products, visit the "La Flor de Jamaica" for a dried chillies tasting, learn to make Fernando's family's Mexican salsa, and finish the three-hour tour off with his mom's homemade mole and a chili-flavored dessert.

Fernando sources the money that he makes on his experience to chillies that are going extinct. "So he, within [himself], is helping his community," Luis remarks. "That's creating more jobs that will go extinct if nobody else was helping. He is doing that and that is what my job is about." Luis is also part of something much bigger than himself; he is supporting community development and positive change in Mexico City and the other communities he served.

Luis often asks hosts like Fernando, "Why do you do what you do?"

The first thing they always say is, "I want to show Mexico in a different light."

Luis regularly flies out to Mexico and Central America to meet with hosts. He connects hosts so they can lift one another up and as a collective, shine a different, authentic light on their home. "You guys could learn more from each other than you can learn from me," Luis reminds the hosts.

Hosts reap the benefit of the community meet-ups. At a gathering Luis hosted in Mexico City, he met an older woman. When Luis was packing up to head home after the two-day event, the woman gave him a big hug, and said, "To me, you're now like a son."

It is like that saying, "help yourself by helping others." In this case it's help your community by helping others. Fernando supports and recognizes his friends at the Jamaican Market. Through donating his earnings to the endangered chillies, he is saving jobs and a piece of his culture. Luis's support elevates the work of Fernando and the women in Mexico City. Sure, Airbnb reaps the benefits as a for-profit company, but so do these communities and individuals sharing their passion and making their homes a more vibrant place to live.

Ingredients

Help yourself and your community by helping others.

Let's band the bands together. Luis gives experience hosts the creative freedom to design their own experiences backing them with the support and connections to maximize their opportunity. Some bands and artists have opted to go the D.I.Y. route and skip working with booking managers and promoters. Some artists, like Drake, have gone as far as to curate their own music festivals. Back in 2010, Drake invited fans to throw down at OVO Fest on his home turf in Toronto, Ontario. Historically the fest takes place at Molson Amphitheater, now called the Budweiser Stage, each summer. Acts like the Weeknd, Eminem, JAY-Z, Kanye West, Lil Wayne, Nas, J. Cole and Kendrick Lamar have made appearances. The fest is named after Drake's label OVO Sound, which supported the fest. He now is backed by Live Nation but the fest lives on, as do all things Drake. Other artists like Justin Vernon of Bon Iver and Aaron Dessner of The National started Eaux Claires Festival to highlight the Midwest regional sounds in their Wisconsin stomping grounds. A lesser known band, Full Service, invites fans to their home in Austin, Texas annually. Full Service Circus is a weekend extravaganza. No animals, just fans camping in the band's backyard, rocking out with Full Service and friends at local venues at night, and hanging by the pool for activities by day. What if there was a central place for all of these artist-curated festivals to live together? Maybe it is the future of Airbnb's very own Music Experience platform. More artists, big and small, could collaborate with artists of different labels, genres, and regions on how to create an engaging experience. Luis said it best when talking to the hosts: "You guys could learn more from each other than you can learn from me." Sure in this book I have gathered a plethora of information on the topic but artists have lived it. Artists, I urge you to use your stories to spark conversation and collaborate with each other.

CHAPTER 17

LIVE MUSIC IS IN A STRANGER'S KITCHEN

———

"Belong anywhere."

Airbnb uses the phrase across marketing materials and plasters it on their headquarters' walls. Yet, the phrase also presents a way to live, serving as a compass for all the work the company does.

Ashley Williams is the Global Host Community Manager of Experiences at Airbnb. The guide for her work is the feeling of belonging. At pasta making classes in Milan, Italy is one place where she says the motto "belong anywhere" is embodied to its full potential.

Pietro's pasta making workshop, while not as flashy as dog sledding in Antarctica, is nonetheless transformative. In his apartment, "you feel like you're part of an Italian family for a day," Ashley says. As she paints the picture, she describes the dramatics of Pietro's mom coming in the kitchen and makes a big fuss in her Italian way as the pasta dries on the patio.

Making pasta with strangers, especially for someone who doesn't like to cook, probably does not sound all that appealing. But Pietro provides much more than a cooking class; he provides Ashley and guests with a magical immersion into another reality and culture through a transformative moment.

* *

Airbnb has invested in building community around their products. They work hard to make sure each community is a healthy one, but community is a natural fit at Airbnb— from homes to experiences.

In other industries, beyond travel and lifestyle, community does not always naturally emerge. It's harder to create a community around a grocery or drug store. For example, how does one feel an affinity Tylenol they pick up when they are under the weather?

The approach Ashely offers brands is to look beyond the product itself when creating community. Community builders must understand:

- What drives their people?
- What interests them?
- What gathers them?

With this knowledge, community managers then can build a group that meets those needs. If you try to fit a square community into a round framework, it is just not going to work.

Honestly answering these questions helps brands discover the purpose of their community. Tylenol would most likely find that sickness drivers their customers and what interests them, as simple as it sounds, is getting better. When people want to get better, they often ask a lot of questions. So what gathers Tylenol customers? Perhaps its an online forum to ask questions when one is sick and where people can share stories of healing.

Tylenol is not the most exciting or sexy example but it proves that you can form a community around any brand with awareness of the customer and their needs. Once you become aware of the customers drive, interest, and point of gathering, then what do you do?

"Building out a mission as either a manifesto or [set of] values so that there's a clear understanding of what banner we're gathering under," Ashley suggests as the next step.

This takes time and careful thought. It is with careful thought that leaders developed "belong anywhere" as Airbnb's manifesto. Guided by the feeling of belonging, the host in Milan was able to help Ashley and other guests feel an affinity with one another and with the Italian culture. When a manifesto is put out into the world, community members are able to incorporate the values into their own personal values. From here, a brand's values manifest into community and a larger story.

Ingredients

Belong anywhere.

Know the purpose of your group and create a manifesto. Figure out what makes your users, or in this case the audience or fans, tick and center the manifesto around that. Ask:

- What is it that makes people come out to concerts?
- What interests and drives these individuals?

Bands with cult followings like the Grateful Dead, Phish, Dave Matthews Band and Pearl Jam have formed tribes of similar kinds of people. But how? Pearl Jam, for example, had some dark and disturbing songs. Songs are analogous to a manifesto. It is the feelings and values surrounding the band that attract the fans. Pearl Jam brought together an angsty group of people. Nirvana manifested a comparable energy, attracting a similar crowd in the 1990s. How do you recreate a manifesto that strong? Is is just through the music?

Josie Dunne is an up-and-coming artist with Atlantic Records. She recently released her first EP "To Be A Little Fish" and hit the road to open for Julia Michaels and Ben Rector. In her Vans, mom jeans, clear rim glasses, and Cubs baseball hat she represented her hometown and felt like her most authentic self. She embodies what she sings in her track "Old School" and as a result, so do her fans. When on tour, she was surprised to find fans "a lot like me, girls in glasses," she jokes.

Queue *Old School* by Josie Dunne

As a young artist, she has utilized Instagram to build her fan base before she took on her first major tour. She posts an "Old School" series covering songs from Aretha Frank-lin and Carl Carlton or early 2000s Beyoncé and Natasha

Bedingfield, which relative to the 21-year-old, is "old school." She sings songs with her bird Calvin on her shoulder or head, embracing her quirky, nerdy self. Her fans strive to embody her vibe.

Josie's image to the world is "old school" on social media, in her recorded and live music, and in real life. Bands and artists that authentically are themselves seem to naturally attract a solid fan base. For emerging artists, the resources of social media in the digital age give them the tools to create a true following before they even step foot on stage. Josie is a fabulous case study of a young woman that follows the beat of her own drum and attracts her tribe through social media. Get those social media followers into a room together and it's electric.

What if more artists were charged by their labels to go beyond promoting their music and high points on social media? Social media often turns into a stream of highlights. What if artists created mini campaigns of who they really are and what they want to be?

Rapper Post Malone could do Tuesday Tatt Talk, explaining the meaning behind his many tattoos. What if Ariana Grande did a cover series of songs by her exes? We all know them after her hit song "Thank U, Next."

Give the fans something to talk and get excited about. Embody the brand, the individual being, and watch the community manifest itself.

CHAPTER 18

LIVE MUSIC IS A NETWORK

ABCD, "Always Be Connecting the Dots." That was the topic of conversation for Aaron Watson on one of his first episodes on his podcast Going Deep back in 2015.

Aaron is a hustler and the founder and CEO of Piper Creatives, a digital agency offering podcasting, event, video and branding services based in Pittsburgh, Pennsylvania. On his podcast he interviews experts in finance and investment, social media and marketing, blockchain, life skills, and writing. On this particular episode he happened to be talking with Larry Gioia, who at the time was serving as a high-level executive at Heist Pricewaterhouse-Coopers (PwC). In the episode, Larry talked about his philosophy of ABCD, which Aaron describes as "opening doors for other people without any expectation of anything in return."

In the early stages of the podcast, Larry did just that for Aaron. He connected the dots and helped Aaron cultivate a network around the brand he was creating.

It was different than most networking situations Aaron had experienced. Aaron says, "It never felt like we were networking or anything that is kind of dirty like that and has a transactional connotation to it." Aaron watched Larry's acts of kindness, backed by the ABCD theory, transform his businesses results.

A year after the podcast aired, Aaron had revisited his conversation with Larry. He thought, "How could we get more people involved and educated on the power of ABCD?"

At their core, Larry and Aaron are connectors. With this strength and mission in mind, they launched a Facebook Group called Connection U. The Facebook group description reads, "Connection U is a group dedicated to scaling the power of 1-to-1 connections. Posts in this group should be: requests for specific intros, celebrations of connections that you've facilitated, and resources that helped you improve your networking."

While there are no rules, there are guidelines that bring acts powered by ABCD to life – be human, be kind, be yourself, and always be connecting the dots. The only requirement of the group is to be human; it is not an exclusive club. The group has over 1,200 members with a shared interest of helping one another.

There is an intentional, real culture that people have bought into at Connection U, and many have reaped its benefits. A woman posted, "I have an absolutely ridiculous ask that there is no shot anyone in this group will be able to help me with but why not give it a shot?"

She had twins graduating college on the same day. They attended two different universities that were a five-hour drive apart from one another or about an hour-long flight. However, her kids did not go to school in close proximity of any commercial airlines. So she shot her shot and asked, "Does anyone have a connection to a private plane that can get me from one campus to the other because one is in the morning and one is in the afternoon?"

Someone bought into the ABCD culture, was inspired by the story, and had the financial means to make it happen. They let her use their private plane and she successfully made it to both of her sons' graduations.

Now, this was a significant request and while great connections are often made through Connection U, they often happen in simple ways that lead to big impact. Aaron's friend, Adam, was building a website repository of naturalist events including hiking, bird watching, and flower identification called Learn Your Land. Through Aaron's work he met Jason, who was creating Active Cities, a website map of where to access sports and recreation in major metropolises— from basketball courts to swimming pools and everything in between. While creating different niches, there was a lot of overlap in the two men's work. So Aaron reached out to the two to see if they would be willing to connect and then sent off an email introduction:

"Hey really excited about this connection! Adam you are going to be able to learn from Jason about how he is using interns to scale, filling of all this data into the map. I know you are just a one man operation so that could be really valuable for you. Jason you are going to be able to learn from Adam how he is using video and other forms of content marketing to raise awareness and brand for Learn Your Land that is going to be able to help you with Active Cities. Hope you two will be able to connect!"

Aaron doesn't always see the final result of these connections and that is not what Connection U is about. It is not about chasing the praise of a newfound business partners, clients or friends. Aaron says, "The chase is that these two people would benefit from knowing one another and that is all it is. There is nothing coming back to me."

With great success online for Connection U, Aaron and Larry brought the online community together in Pittsburgh for a meetup.

Meetups are open to all. They are simple, as the name implies, people meeting up. With no agenda or hero speaker drawing in a crowd, the space is simply set up for people to come as they are. People arrive with the pure intention to connect with others. It was well worth the trek for Olga and many other Connection U members.

Connection U is, in Aaron's words, "a real web of people that give a shit about one another and give first without expectations." It is one thing to give and another to forget.

Give first.

Forget the shit.

Ingredients

Set the expectation that there is no expectation – that is what ABCD is all about.

This is a tricky one with live music because people want to know what they are spending their money on. A lot of times they want the star power in the room. They want to know where they are going, who is going to be there, if there will be drinks or food, and what they are paying for. Why pay for a country concert if you really like rock? Sofar Sounds plays off expectations well. When people buy tickets for a Sofar show in their city, they do not know what building or even what part of town the show will be in in some cases. Twenty-four hours before the show, the address is released but the artists are still a mystery. There are no details to create expectations around the audience or music. However, people still buy tickets and shows sell out. How? With Connection U, people show up because they know at the bare minimum they are getting human connection, that is what they are promised even if it is in a weird part of town and there is no keynote speaker or workshop offering key takeaways. At Sofar, you might have an odd venue or artist you don't totally connect with, but at least you know you are going to hear live music from three different groups. At both Connection U and Sofar, they have set that expectation to set aside expectations, leaving space for excitement, surprise, and spontaneity.

CHAPTER 19

LIVE MUSIC IS A CULT

Why do people go to Mass every Sunday? Why do some people stick to the same bar every weekend? Why do some people always buy Apple phones or Converse shoes or cars made by Ford?

Why are people committed to things?

That is the question that Douglas Atkins asked on repeat during his career immersed in the world of advertising. Douglas spent the first half of his career in New York working on brands of household names like JetBlue, Lipitor and Mercedes.

After one long day in the office, at a time when Douglas's clients started to believe marketing was dead because "all products were the same," he sat in a focus group of kids talking about their favorite brand of sneakers. They talked in evangelical terms about Converse shoes. These kids felt an affinity to a piece of rubber and fabric that they wore on their feet. How could someone show a commitment to an inanimate object, a mundane commodity? While Douglas's clients said "marketing was dead," everything these kids were saying proved the opposite. The Converse-loving kids behaved with extreme brand loyalty and commitment to the shoes.

Douglas found fascination in the cult following that Converse had developed. He wondered how other top brands had created a similar following.

Take the Apples and Harley Davidsons of the world. Douglas looked to answer why people are so committed to touch-screen smartphones with a shiny fruit logo on the back, and why people are committed to riding on a motorized bicycle made in Milwaukee, Wisconsin. Why are people committed to Apple and Harley when they have other options?

In his research he talked to not only cult brands and their customers, but also members of true cults. Douglas interviewed hundreds of members of cults from Krishna to

Scientology, decoding why people believe what they do and why people find a sense of belonging where they do.

Douglas's findings captured the idea of "It is not where you go, it is who you are with." It's exciting, comforting, and inviting to share an idea or common interest with others.

The question still remains, could people's commitment to their iPhones really be the same kind of commitment cult members have to their lifestyle that seems so obscure to outsiders?

Turns out people's commitment to iPhones, iPads, iPods, and iEverything is parallel to cult members commitment to their perspective ideology.

"If committed belonging was totally related just to cults and people who join cults were not like normal people, then it wouldn't have been worthy of studying because there wouldn't have been an edge case. But the truth is that when I talked to people who are from Scientology, from Krishna, from Apple, from Harley Davidson they all exhibited the same feelings, attitudes and behaviors around why they wanted to belong to this group and what it did for them," Douglas said. "It didn't matter who I was interviewing. The reasons for believing and belonging were nearly always the same."

With these shared feelings, attitudes, and behaviors cults come together in one accord. Yet, in a way that seems totally contradictory, people were able to become more themselves as members of their cult community. Douglas calls it the "cult paradox," explaining that individuals become more themselves and more individualistic in these groups because "there's a sense of safety by being amongst others."

Community is defined by the Oxford English dictionary as "a group of people living in the same place or having a particular characteristic in common."[50] Nowhere does it say anything explicit about belonging or commitment. Sure, there is the community one is born into and there is no choice in that. In the home community, people have some shared experience and shared sense of geography. However, what Douglas has found to be the glue in highly functioning communities, cults being the strongest, is interaction that leads to the formation of relations and ultimately feelings of attachment and mutual responsibility.

Douglas's research pushed him out of his advertising career and into building community. He shifted his gaze from extreme forms of community to everyday, regular forms of community. Community can be formed and is formed around ordinary things like tea, running, dogs, and yes, music. Douglas transitioned into the role of chief community officer at MeetUp.com, a platform that connects people to gather together in real life to share a cup of tea, go on a long run, have a doggy date, or jam together.

Douglas asked the same question again: "Why are people committed to this thing?" (the thing being the MeetUp community that they spend time with). He found whether people showed up for belly dancing or to practice Spanish, if they showed up four or more times, they became a highly committed and valued member of the group.

On behalf of MeetUp Douglas would ask, "Why did you show up?" to belly dancers and beginner Spanish speakers.

The first answer was not, "I found other people who share the same interests."

Instead it was, "I made new friends " or "I found people who like me."

When people approach a new situation, social anxiety floods us with questions. If I go to a MeetUp for singers on my own, it is my natural tendency to start asking myself all sorts of questions and work myself up.

"Are these people cool? Are they boring? Are they going to be weird? Are they going to be classically trained or just in it for the fun?"

"Will they think I am cool? Or boring? Or weird? Will they think I am a bad singer? Will they think I have bad taste in music?"

There are a multitude of questions that overtake my brain in these situations that Douglas simplified into two categories: "Are these people like me?" and "Will they like me?"

Once I find common ground with fellow singers, based on the notion of "we are all in this together," I am able to surpass the first anxiety due to being in a space with like-minded people. On to the second anxiety, whether I will be accepted. In these moments I, as Douglas has observed many others do, ramp up my social skills, empathy, and look for points of connection.

With enough practice sharing and working to understand the feelings of others in these new, seemingly awkward situations, I can join the "extreme empaths" club, a group of people who have the gift of sensing the emotional and mental state of those around them. Take Roberto for example, he exemplifies someone who works hard to be an "extreme empath."

Roberto lives in New York City. Aside from his day job, he hosts a listing on Airbnb's website. A normal day in the chaos that is New York City, life can be quite hard. When a reminder of a guest's arrival appears on his phone in late afternoon, he remembers, 'Oh no, I've got to check someone in at 5:00 p.m. tonight and they've just flown from Israel' or wherever they may be coming from.

Whatever emotions New York cast upon him that day, "I ramp up my hostiness," Roberto says. "Hostiness" is the term to describe Roberto's welcoming nature, curiosity to find commonality, and yes, the ability to empathize.

Roberto jokes, "It sort of made me into a better person because I am more hosty more of the time now."

With empathy Roberto turns an estranged New York City into a short-term home for guests, MeetUp hosts turn like-minded individuals into friends, Apple turns consumers into loyal brand customers, and Scientology turns people into devoted followers. Loyal brand followers sound worlds apart from cult members at first glance but Douglas proves that in practice, they are not all that different. Human beings are just looking for something to believe in and a place to belong.

Ingredients

Embody the "extreme empath" so people can believe and belong.

What if not only artists and venue hosts ramped up their hostiness, but so did fans among their fellow concertgoers? Concertgoers are called to be "extreme empaths," sensing the emotional and mental state of those around them so that they can engage with them. Fans can express this same empathy to the artist in the way they focus on the energy and emotion of the music. Start with the basics: listen intently when the performance is rolling, say hi to the person next to you in between sets, dance and sing along when the mood is right. Take your "extreme empathy" to the next level: ask yourself what the song is about, ask the person next to you why they came to the show, and keep the dance party or music or whatever mood the show entails alive when you leave the venue. Support the artists by following them on social media, coming back to see them when they are in your city, and sending their new tunes along to fellow music lovers. These are the kind of actions that bring artists to the next level.

CHAPTER 20

LIVE MUSIC IS
A COMMUNAMANTRA

The phrase "we all live here" disrupted Rich Alapack's entire life in 2015.

He was walking down the street in his Chicago neighborhood with his dog Benson, reflecting on his day's work as a creative and brand strategist at Tumblr. He was feeling discouraged by the negative comments he had heard people making about Chicago, the city he called home, in his everyday conversations with people both globally and locally. Rich felt like a nag correcting people on their ignorant comments about race and other social issues. It seemed as though too many things have evolved into reasons for he and others should not to get along.

As a high schooler, he felt more comfortable addressing these comments head-on. His senior year, Rich moved from Canada to his cousin's home in Minnesota to pursue his dream of playing baseball. Classmates made seemingly harmless racial comments; Rich recalled, "People were so casually hateful in their comments," which he was not used to at home.

While it felt uncomfortable at times, Rich found the courage to speak up and address these comments, recognizing that they were not harmless and that it was important to stand up for marginalized people. He wasn't afraid to approach and correct the prom queen or the biggest jocks at the time. In high school, these comments came infrequently, but as he was creating a career for himself in Chicago, they seemed to come up in conversation often.

As Rich reflected on this, he and Benson strolled by a white wall in their neighborhood that had never been tagged. He thought, "What could I write on that wall, that if I did, it might not need to be removed?"

The phrase "we all live here" popped into his head, encompassing the equality that he so desired to see in his community.

In big, bold, colorful lettering he wrote the words "we all live here" on the white wall. He took the mantra to other Chicagoans to see if they would adopt it, printed signs that read in bold black ink "we all live here" and asked strangers to hold them in pictures at community events around the city. They appreciated the slogan, proudly grabbed onto the sign and posed for a photo with it. He turned this series of photos into a Tumblr blog.

As his movement picked up momentum, Rich thought to himself, "In a city and country so divided, I felt like I could use my creativity for a bigger purpose."

Soon schools caught wind of what he was doing. A teacher friend asked Rich to speak with his high school Media Studies class. Energy was high on the high school campus after her spoke an article was shared in the school paper, and he was invited to come back. This time he was given the chance to do something with the phrase for the entire student body. He created a curriculum for the schools centered around art, community and technology, ACT for short. The mission of the ACT School Program is to "work with schools to conceive, plan, construct, and unveil a unique public art project incorporating our phrase 'we all live here' for each participating school."

One class speaking engagement snowballed into a school wide ACT program and led Rich to launch the ACT program at 55 schools in the first year of the project and 89 schools in the second year. It became clear that there was an urgency for Rich's message and a demand for his voice in schools. Quickly his side hustle took over and he left his job at Tumblr to pursue the ACT Program full time.

The message Rich imparts on students in the program is one of great integrity. He tells them, "When you hear someone say something hateful, you can argue with them, but the argument is going to go nowhere because the hateful person wasn't using logic or reason anyways." In this situation, it becomes more about winning the argument rather than the subject matter. Perpetrators often fail to listen, missing the point no matter how intelligent it may be.

So Rich proposes another way to address the situation, "Instead, what if we try and just say, 'we all live here' and walk away from that person." There doesn't have to be an argument or a clash rather, this phrase has the power to stop people in their tracks and make them think. School age children are taught to use the phrase "we all live here" as peaceful ammunition in an argument. It's powerful when a child schools an adult and teaches them a lesson in humanity. The phrase has power to transform and is displayed as public art in many Chicago neighborhoods as a reminder, planting a seed of doubt in the hate.

Rich recognized that kids, on a basic level, care about sports, arts, music, fashion, and maybe their toys. These are the main ingredients of a kid's life. When they are brought to participate in Rich's public art projects, they are proud to be part of it. They are excited to share and say, "I did that" and be a part of the conversation. This project does more than provide kids with a creative outlet; it also shapes their mindset. It doesn't just leave an imprint on the people these kids interact with, it also leaves an impression on anyone that passes by the art and sees it.

A Mantra & The Spark of a Movement

Just as individuals adopt mottos or mantras that guide the way they live their best life, Rich had created a mantra for the city of Chicago, a *communamantra* if you will. Rich defines *communamantra* as "a positive, publicly visible uniting statement that expresses community's basic beliefs." *Communamantras* have been used by other cities to rekindle their spirits and inspire change.

In the 1970s, Mitlon Glaser designed the iconic "I <3 New York" logo to heal the failing New York City by creating a buzz around tourism. He created the advertising campaign pro bono in hopes to help his city rise and thrive again. At the time, the city was on the verge of bankruptcy, companies were laying off a sixth of their workers, neighborhoods were deteriorating, and crime was at an all time high. The campaign rekindled the flame for hometown pride and shifted the public mentality toward being better neighbors. It was with this pride and drive that a new wave of tourism emerged in the city, but even more monumental was the revitalization of infrastructure and the sense of camaraderie that resurfaced. They got tired of the community they were living in and took action, inspired by this art that united them.

In defining community Rich says, "the place is just as important as the idea and they're sort of intertwined things, which is why I think they share the same word." New York as a community is defined by skyscrapers, its five boroughs, and its East Coast location as much as it is defined by the "I <3 NY" tagline.

The same is true for Chicago, defined by the character of its 77 neighborhoods, ties to the river, and Midwest roots. The way the idea "we all live here" had intertwined with the physical makeup of the Chicago community has been a special feature that might not have worked in another community.

Art Initiates Conversation

"Art has a unique ability to reach people when words fail," Rich says.

Art aligns people on topics that are difficult to initiate conversation around. Back in October 2018 Rich collaborated on a public art display with Apple on Michigan Avenue. Along the Magnificent Mile, Rich transformed the Apple plaza into an emoji wonderland recreating twenty-five, 12-foot by 12-foot emojis on the plaza.

"Watching that happen all around me in the middle of downtown Chicago with a bunch of people that saw me give a talk inside the store, but then a bunch more people that just happen to be walking by and decided they wanted to join in with no idea really what was going on, was incredible," Rich explains. In one of the highest foot traffic destinations in Chicago, the "here" of "we all live here" can be representative of the city as a whole or of the block the project is taking place at.

While "we all live here" is Rich's cry to end hatred, the phrase is designed to be open-ended regarding what "here" is who "we" are, and what "live" means. To some, "we all live here" is a call to be stewards to the earth at their local park by picking up trash. To others it is a call to end violence by showing love to their neighbors, and to others it is a call to be an advocate for equality by becoming a government official in the city.

However people define "we all live here," it is important they do it for themselves.

It is more fulfilling if people find, as Rich says, "a way that leverages whatever makes them unique. I call that... people's superpowers." The superpowers can be the change they wish to see in the world. Maybe your superpower is art and branding like Rich or perhaps it has nothing to do with art. Maybe it is math, science, or creative problem-solving. What makes you uniquely you?

"We all live here" and we are called to use our superpowers to meet our community's greatest needs.

Ingredients

Channel Superpowers

It's all about knowing your why, your purpose. Why do you do what you do? Why get up every day and do it? Most importantly, why you? What's your asset?

Some questions to think about:

- To the music experience organizers – What's your value proposition? Who is on your team? Why are they on your team? What are their superpowers?
- To the music performers – What makes you uniquely you as an artist? Is it your vocals? Guitar skills? Presence in performance? Or is it totally unrelated to the music? Is it your nerdy love for the environment?
- To the concertgoer – Why do you go to concerts? Why do you go to community events? What types of events attract you? What do you like to do most at the events? What do you bring to the event? Your expertise on a topic? Energy? Personality? A talet?

Know your superpower and lean in.

- To the music experience organizer – If you have the best photographers but your video production team is lacking, capitalize on what you have. Don't worry that you have gaps in video production for now. Get to the next level in what you are already good at and don't worry about your weakness just yet.
- To the music performers – If your strength is performance, adopt the Blues Brothers way, put on a show and make it a theatrical production. If it is your nerdy love for the environment, talk about it! Share what is uniquely you.

- To the concertgoer – If you are a chatterbox, start a conversation with the person next to you. If you're the observer and the chatterbox starts the conversation with you, bring it to the next level. Share what insight you are collecting to inspire deeper thought in those around you.

Communamantra

Sometimes friends, girlfriends, boyfriends, or family members drag people to shows. Just as people define "we all live here" differently, people all go to concerts for different reasons. Take a step back and define a basic, shared community belief. It's simple, people attend concerts for live music. An all-encompassing *comunamantra* for a live music experience could be something like "we are all here" for a night of live music. In this we must remember and honor that where "here" is, who "we" are, and what "live" means is different for every person in the room.

CHAPTER 21

LIVE MUSIC IS A HOTEL LOBBY AND A TOWN HALL

———

La Grange, Illinois is a charming suburb fifteen miles west of Chicago. Historic homes are mixed in with new modern construction in walking distance of schools, parks, the library, and the Metra train, the passageway to the Windy City. In the traditional downtown business district you will find residents and visitors milling the streets on coffee runs and in between workout classes, grabbing goods from the local hardware store, dining out, grabbing a drink, or heading to see the latest movie. The La Grange Business Association is a resource for all things La Grange – arts and entertainment, shopping, dining and service businesses.

"Our business is to help you build yours," the association boasts as their mission.

Throughout the year they put on holiday walks, festivals, and programming that enhance the economic vitality of La Grange for business owners and bring the residents together in community.

Nancy Cummings is the executive director of the La Grange Business Association, making a name for La Grange as a business hub and a destination for day tourism. Nancy spent her early career in hospitality with Hyatt Hotels and draws upon that knowledge in the way she builds the local community.

"When I am thinking about La Grange, I always think of Village Hall as the hotel lobby," Nancy says. The residents as the sleeping rooms, the restaurants as a big food court, the retailers as the gift shop, and public works as the conventions services department."

A town is a strikingly good analogy to the intricate hotel complex.

"In the hotel industry you were trained as an employee that if there was a scrap of paper on the floor, you pick it up. It did not matter if you were the regional vice president, a steward or a cocktail server. If there was a gum wrapper on the floor, you would pick it up," Nancy adds. We see Nancy's work continue to translate from her time in hotels as she says, "Even now, I will walk down the street and there will be a napkin flying around and I feel obligated to go chase after it."

Care is at the root of Nancy's actions in the way she interacts with the environment of La Grange, the business owners, and the residents. Care happens to be at the core of the Hyatt Hotel's mission, which reads "We care for people so they can be their best."

It's with selflessness and humility that Nancy played her part to make Hyatt home for guests during their stay. It is with her continued grace and hospitality that she makes La Grange a thriving place to own a business and to live.

Ingredients

Care enough to pick up the trash.

Nancy does and so should you.

The village has a maintenance crew whose job is to make sure the streets of La Grange are clean. Nowhere in Nancy's job description does it say "pick up trash as seen walking through the streets on and off the clock." Yet, she does it and feels obligated to do so. Music festivals and concerts are known for leaving the venue cluttered with empty beer cans and the dirty evidence of a good time. Lollapalooza is among the music festivals that runs programs like Rock & Recycle. Festival goers are invited to take a garbage bag and collect recycling throughout the weekend. Fans who recycle are rewarded with swag for their contribution.

The bags started a conversation around sustainability and have created an impact.

In 2018, Chicago Lollapaloozers and staff diverted 145.6 tons of waste by recycling and composting.[51] What if they had sent out artist to help the fans pick up? Is it a PR stunt to send artists out to pick up recycling with fans? Yes. Does it make sense? Well that depends on who the artist is.

If it is Dave Matthews Band, why not send them into the crowd to help with the recycling at the end of the night? The band has been at the forefront of the environmental movement in the musician community. Some may forget the band has a green thumb after their little incident in 2004 when 800 pounds of human waste was dumped from their tour bus into the

Chicago River and partially onto a tourist boat below. However, back in 1999 the band established Bama Works Fund to support charitable programs primarily in their home of Charlottesville, VA. The fund has since raised over $52 million that has served community needs locally, nationally and internationally.[52] The band really got into the green scene when they launched their Bama Green Project and partnered with Reverb, a nonprofit dedicated to empowering millions of individuals united around music to take action for a better future for people and the planet. On tour in the summer of 2010 the band's fans were inspired to volunteer, showing up early for the show to learn more about the ecological justice and to help set up the Eco-Village recycling, water and information stations. They got some new knowledge, helped the cause and rocked out with the band for free. The Bama Green Project still educates fans on simple, positive ways to take environmental action and makes an effort to neutralize the environmental impact the band makes on the road, in the studio and at home. So if you are an artist like Dave Mattews and believe in sustainability, make a statement and join the crowd to take action. If as an artists sustainability is not the cause you are passionate about, don't fake it. Find other "garbage" you can pick up by aligning your voice with social issues you are passionate about. Show you care by getting down and dirty picking up the trash in whatever forms it comes in. Know the little actions add up, whether they're done by Dave in center stage or by the fan in the last row.

PART 3

LIVE MUSIC EXPERIENCE: RECIPE & TASTING GUIDE

Now you have traveled on sea and land to experience a slice of the most unique, authentic, raw, live music experiences. You then stepped outside the box to digital detox camp and a pasta making class for lessons beyond the music space in creating community. A set of ingredients to cook up the ultimate live music experience lay before you.

So now what?

To the chef, the promoter, venue owner, concert host, artist, band, and event organizer, in Chapter 23 of this section you will find a recipe that details the perfect blend for fostering community in live music experiences.

To our hungry (perhaps hangry at this point) friends, the fans, in Chapter 24 of this section you will find the tasting guide for the most savory of experiences. Like fine wine or a five-course meal, a lot of time and energy is put into creating the ultimate music experience for you. The tasting guide provides the tools to expand your palate and enjoy the finer things in life.

We are LIVE, it's cooking time!

CHAPTER 22

ULTIMATE RECIPE FOR LIVE MUSIC EXPERIENCES

In a five-star restaurant, chefs have the resources, and more importantly the experience, to cook up an unforgettable dishes. In a college house kitchen, the chef, a generous term for most college students, often has to get a little more creative in what they cook up, but the meal can still be memorable.

Whatever your chef status is in the kitchen, you must know your ingredients and understand how they blend. The ultimate recipe for you, the chef of live music experiences, calls you to:

- Awareness of these ingredients
- Purpose in the blending
- Creativity in the presentation

In the scope of music, the five-star restaurant represents the bucket-list venues of the world – the Red Rocks, Madison Square Gardens, Sydney Opera Houses, and Radio City Musical Halls. However, this recipe is for those of you cooking in the college kitchens – the overlooked space perfect for making memories.

* *

HERE IS THE ULTIMATE LIVE LIVE! RECIPE:

What you will need:

Physical Space. In part one of this book we saw how many different spaces were transformed to bands' and musicians' center stage. On the cruise deck, in homes, and in the birthplace of rock and roll, there is an opportunity for music to live and community to belong. In true adventurous spirits, the chef is challenged to look at each space with open eyes and possibility as the venue for their next curated music gig. In the very first chapter we learned you must call it what you want and own it when the city of Austin proclaimed itself as the Musical Capital of the World. The same confidence is needed when a living room, mountaintop, or any weird and wonderful space is the musical venue for the night. It doesn't have to be a historically prescribed place for music like Schubas if you call it what you want and own it. Know your assets, understand the hurdles, and create a strategy backed by leaders to communicate that this is where the live music is and the community belongs for the evening.

Ingredients for the Chef:

Treat everyone like a friend. Think about skipping the tickets at the door and go with a guest list. People want to be recognized as a unique individual rather than a number, so treat them like one. Embody your "extreme empath" and ramp up your hospitality to help others feel welcome.

Super serve the ecosystem. Thank everyone you lay eyes on you and listens to the music – venue owners, the sound people, lighting team, hospitality, and yes, the fans. Andy at Sixthman went as far as giving gifts for the sound guys and writing thank you notes for the fans. It doesn't have to be elaborate. A simple, thoughtful gesture makes anyone feel like a star.

Foster community wherever you go. The beauty of groups like Sofar Sounds and Side Door is that they provide music lovers with the toolbox and the autonomy to create a community-centric music experience that captures a slice of their local culture. Sofar Sounds provides another layer, a global community. With this global community is the invitation to experience music in a ritualized, intimate, unique setting in over 400 cities around the world. Joining a network like this is the secret sauce for an intimate community to be a part of a bigger narrative.

Lean into the culture. We see this with the Airbnb experience – AFROHAUS Brunch, Chillies with an Expert, and pasta making in Milan. Visitors are given the keys to belong anywhere. Ask yourself, what is it that makes people come out to the type of show I am putting on? What interests and drives these individuals? Don't try to get everyone to come out, just get the people that fit with the environment and the culture you are fostering. Know your purpose and capitalize on it.

Collaboration. The Rock and Roll Hall of Fame exemplified internal and external collaboration that brought a swell of energy to their events and a new vibrancy to the city's dynamic. Collaboration is the key to add the most value to an experience; it's an avenue to adding great depth to the showcase when artists advocate for the greater good, and it's the means to capturing the unique local experience. It's everything from the art on the walls to the food and drink for sale during the show to the storytelling between songs. Each piece adds a rich layer to the experience.

Stop them in their tracks. This was the biggest lesson from the buskers and street performers, Ryan O'Reilly and the people Billy Ferguson met on the Unknown tour. They honed their craft on the street, which gave them a special edge— the X factor— on stage. The product (music), price (free), place (the streets) and promotion (singing songs and selling CDs) have challenged street performers to stop people in the business of everyday life to experience an unscheduled performance. Take that same energy and captivation to the stage for a performance that fans seek out. It can be electric.

No walls. On a Sixthman cruise, walls come down quite naturally as bands and fans wander off into paradise. In other settings, the mix of media gives the audience perspective to peel back the layers of character and personality of bands and artists. Bringing together music, art, storytelling, and games important and relevant to a band's identity allows fans to immerse themselves into a rich experience.

Ritual. This is a powerful ingredient to bring purpose and reflection to routine. At Sofar the ritual manifests in the way the MC introduces each act. For artists like Maggie Rogers it is closing out each show with "I Wanna Dance with Some-body," the ultimate tune for moving and grooving. There is a level of predictability that provides comfort and an invitation into a ceremony of sorts that is nostalgic.

Prescribed movement. People are awkward, so tell them what to do. Tell them to clap their hands, dance, and talk to the people next to them. People need the invitation to be vulnerable and for many people, dancing and talking to strangers is very vulnerable.

Choose your own adventure. Every genre of music calls for a different type of atmosphere that invites people in for something different – be it dancing, singing along, head nodding, toe tapping, simple listening or straight up raging. In the intimate setting you can label it that way – "dance show" or "acoustic set" – so fans can then "choose their own adventure" and move at their own speed, in their own style. Take it a step further and do a set of fan favorites and another of songs that didn't make the record. Make it clear what the show has in store and the right people will end up in the room.

Communamantra. Create a manifesto of why you are gathering. Make it loud, proud, and crystal clear. Make sure it is inclusive and all-encompassing of those you gather, much like "we all live here" is for the city of Chicago or "I <3 NY"

is for New York City. Define the basic community belief asso-
ciated with attending your live music event.

Pick up the trash. Literally – start a community initiative
that anyone can participate in like Rock and Recycle at Lollapalooza. The initiative is for a bigger cause and something
in which all fans can make progress with simple action—
picking up trash. But this idea of "picking up the trash" has
a bigger meaning. It calls people to step up beyond their job
title and get their hands a little dirty. In creating these musical experiences, you will likely wear many hats and some that
may seem "lower" than your job title. Just do it.

Instructions:

Start with understanding the space you are working with.
Define it, own it, and communicate it. Each genre and experience is going to call for a different combination of the ingredients from above. Sift through the ingredients that naturally
fit with your genre. From there, take the ingredients and
start experimenting. See what makes the experience sweeter
and what might be better left on the shelf for another time.
Always follow these simple guidelines:

- Awareness of these ingredients
- Purpose in the blending
- Creativity in the presentation

CHAPTER 23

ULTIMATE TASTING GUIDE TO LIVE MUSIC EXPERIENCES

When you were a little kid, what food did you hate most? Do you still hate it? Maybe broccoli? When your mom would put it on the table as a kid you were gagging but then one day, you found yourself in a situation where it would be rude not to eat the food in front of you. You tried it and it was not all that bad. Then you had broccoli a second time, sauteed in garlic and butter and you thought, "Wow, what have I been doing all this time." Perhaps with a little age and perspective the food you despised most grew on you. With that same fresh perspective and openness to try something new, your live music experience will be more flavorful.

Whether you are a seasoned concert veteran or a music lover looking for a fresh new scene, the tasting guide calls you to:

- Openness to the unknown
- Intention in your presence
- Return of energy

We are tasting something a little different than your mama's meatloaf. The tasting guide opens your palate to experiences jam-packed full of flavor that will make your taste buds go wild, or in the case of music, your ears and eyes.

* *

HERE IS YOUR ULTIMATE TASTING GUIDE TO LIVE LIVE!

Keep in mind:

It is not about the star in the room. Often times that's why we show up. It's natural to buy into the hype. Know though that the opener who you might not be all that excited about was specially picked because they relate to the main act, the person you came to see. Give them a shot. Take a look around the room while you are there. You and all the people around you show up to these experiences for the same reason, music. Sure there is some variance, some people get dragged along by their significant other or perhaps they're simply looking for something to do. But start a conversation in between sets and learn about those around you. Your conversation might be better than the main act.

This is a celebration of life and art. If you celebrate, others will follow. That is what Jillian Richards learned when she brought back the lessons in intentional, community-centric living to New York City after Camp Grounded. If the room calls for it, get a little goofy and invite others into it. If the room calls for more attention, be attentive and set the example. Celebrate the life and art by matching the artist's energy.

It's not polite to take more than you give. An artist is up their putting their heart and soul into their craft, giving their energy to you. Do them a favor, give some of it back. It doesn't have to be in the form of raging like a crazy person, but if the mood calls for it, by all means go for it. Be mindful of your intentions for going to the show and be attentive to the experience. It's a lot more fun when everyone buys in.

You might want to ditch technology. Before the start of a theatrical production the crowd is reminded to turn their phone off and in entering many museums, patrons are reminded to not take pictures. We are called to honor the art in these settings. At concerts, we must not overlook that the band or musician performing is an artist that deserves to be honored and celebrated just like actors, actresses, painters, and sculptors. Sneak a quick picture or video of the band on stage, then put your phone away and tag them later. Tagging artists is important for their success and growth. In traditional venue settings, the first thing they look at when booking artists is their social following. Your comments, likes, tags, and follows do count. Your energy counts too, don't forget that. So focus on the main act and focus on where your feet are— the present moment.

You can choose your adventure. Know that adventure does not mean jumping out of airplanes or walking a tightrope between skyscrapers. Instead, adventure is a mindset. It's looking at each day, each experience, as a possibility. So if you are invited to a show in a tool shed, antique shop or a stranger's living room, you must move into this adventurous mindset. Buy into the possibility of these weird venues and meet artists where they are in a given moment in time.

Going LIVE, It's Tasting Time!

At your next concert or live music experience, try one of the tasting tips. Pay extra attention to the opener, ditch your phone, or ask the person next to you, "What brought you here tonight?" You are in control of your own experience. Remember Live LIVE! calls you to:

- Open to the unknown
- Intention in your presence
- Return of energy

CONCLUSION

Turns out my Woodstock is not just about music, it's a way of life.

The way I make sense of the world is through going out and Living LIVE!

Live LIVE!

/liv līv/

to remain present in the vibrancy of the given experience

not aimless; on a purposeful adventure

Writing this book was an experience, an experiment in entrepreneurship and a personal journey. The greatest lessons to how, as a human being, you and I can Live LIVE! lies is in between the lines of the text you just read. The lessons were in the process.

The process was energizing at one moment and paralyzing the next. Here is what I learned:

- I am energized by learning
- I am not an expert in the music space
- I am not an author, I am a creator

What do I mean?

I am energized by learning.

My favorite part of the process was chasing after innovators and picking their brain on what an intimate show is and what it could be. I found myself in black holes of the internet with no end in sight reading psychology articles, discovering different creative platforms, and studying thought leaders. As I write the final pages of this book, it feels as though the journey is just beginning. The more I learned, the bigger this topic seemed to be. A theme that emerged when researching how to foster community was design. I am excited to dive into and learn more about design thinking, a process of creative problem solving that focuses on people and practicing empathy when creating a product.

I am not an expert in the music space.

This is one tiny snippet of what the music industry – a very complex, multidimensional space – entails. There were people that I talked to that have dedicated their entire lives to working in the industry and honed a very technical craft along the way. I took a very generalist approach to the innovative end of the live music experience. The book you read was a reflection of experiences, conversations, and findings in a quick nine months time.

I am not an author, I am a creator.

The way I make sense of information is not writing in story form. The writing and editing stage of the book was overwhelming to me at times. While I learned writing in this format is not the medium for me to best make sense of information, I came close to the medium right for me. Just as I found that one of the most powerful things that a music experience creator can do is mix media – music, art, storytelling, and games – I found that to be true in my own creation process. A combination of photo, voice recording, graphic designing, and short, tongue and cheek, poetic written pieces is my style. So stay tuned for my next project! You can follow @oconnell_ko on Instagram or check out my website, www.ventureko.com, to stay up to date.

These are the areas I feel I can Live LIVE! This is where I found my own Woodstock, a place where I can connect to talented artists and purposeful people that excite me in all aspects of my creative and spiritual life.

So here is your call to Live LIVE!

To you the chef – the promoter, venue owner, concert host, artist, band, and event organizer

May the Ultimate Recipe be a call to intentionally create a music experience that lights the souls of the group you gather on fire.

To you the hungry patron – the fans and concertgoers

May the Tasting Guide serve you your perfect Woodstock in your hometown, in your local clubs, with your favorite music, and with a group of strangers or a group of friends.

To you the human – yes, you, _insert your name here_!

May this book serve as your call to Live LIVE! in your everyday life. Remain present in the vibrancy of the present experience and not aimless. Life is one big purposeful adventure. May the lessons in the stories, the ingredients they offer, the ultimate recipe and tasting guide be a framework for a space much bigger than music.

Go forth and Live LIVE!

Go Out & Live LIVE!

Did you enjoy the experiences you just read about? Looking for an intimate music experience in your city? A kind of show that brings engagement to the next level?

If you are looking to discover something new and make a new friend in the process, check out Sofar Sounds – https://www.sofarsounds.com/

If you are looking to get the local flare of the city you are in and a true cultural immersion check out Airbnb Concerts – https://bit.ly/2Xooo1a

If you are looking to dance combining music and wellness, check out Daybreaker – https://www.daybreaker.com/

Want more?

Every city has their own music scene waiting to be discovered in corner bars, coffee shops, historic venues, and in homes. Use the internet to get off the internet – Google "live music near me." Check out a show in your neighborhood and talk to people. The more people you talk to, the closer you'll get to the true musical beat in your city.

WORKS REFERENCES

———

INTRODUCTION

1   "All Things Considered." 2009. Podcast. Demetri Martin On 'Taking Woodstock.' https://www.npr.org/templates/story/story.php?storyId=111922789.

2   "Millennials: Fueling The Experience Economy." 2017. Eventbrite US. https://www.eventbrite.com/blog/academy/millennials-fueling-experience-economy/.

3   Jack Ma On The Future Of Education (Teamwork Included). 2018. Video. https://www.youtube.com/watch?v=rHt-5-RyrJk.

4   Ibid.

PART 1: LIVE MUSIC: INGREDIENTS FROM WITHIN

5   Kurzgesagt – In a Nutshell. 2019. Loneliness. Video. https://www.youtube.com/watch?time_continue= 30&v=n3Xv_g3g-mA.

6   Suttie, Jill. 2015. "Four Ways Music Strengthens Social Bonds." Greater Good. https://greatergood.berkeley.edu/article/ item/four_ways_music_strengthens_social_bonds.

7   Ibid.

8   Ibid.

9   "Live Nation Entertainment Reports Fourth Quarter And Full Year 2018 Results - Live Nation Entertainment." 2019. Live Nation Entertainment. https://www.livenationen-tertainment.com/2019/02/live-nation-entertainment-re-ports-fourth-quarter-and-full-year-2018-results/.

CHAPTER 1

10 TED. 2018. *How To Build A Thriving Music Scene In Your City.* Image. https://www.ted.com/talks/elizabeth_ cawein_we_built_this_city_on_a_bold_music_identity/ up-next?language=en.

11 Ibid.

12 Ibid.

13 Ibid.

14 Ibid

CHAPTER 2

15 "The Four Ps Of Marketing." 2019. Purely Branded. https://www.purelybranded.com/insights/the-four-ps-of-marketing/.

CHAPTER 4

16 *The Unknown Tour*. 2018. Video. https://www.theunknowntour.com/videos.

17 Ibid.

18 Ibid.

19 Ibid.

20 Reid, Thomas. 1969. Essays on the intellectual powers of man. Cambridge, Mass: M.I.T. Press.

21 Glei, Jocelyn. 2019. "The Problem With The "What Else?" Mindset." *Jocelyn K. Glei*. https://jkglei.com/what-else/.

CHAPTER 5

22 Landis, John, Robert K. Weiss, John Belushi, Dan Aykroyd, James Brown, Cab Calloway, Ray Charles, et al. 2005. The Blues Brothers. Universal City, CA: Universal.

CHAPTER 6

23 Brett Newski. 2018. *Band Gets KICKED OUT Of Wal-Mart || DORK ROCK BUM RUSH!!!*. Video. https://www.youtube.com/watch?v=llnwfnBsAmo.

24 Robert, Kolker. 2002. "Seeing The Possibilities." *Oprah.Com*. https://www.oprah.com/spirit/seeing-the-possibilities/all.

CHAPTER 8

25 TEDx Talks. 2017. *Making Music History… One Living Room At A Time | Rafe Offer | Tedxlondonbusinessschool*. Image. https://www.youtube.com/watch?v=2-rLU4l6HdY.

26 Ibid.

27 Ibid.

28 Ibid.

CHAPTER 9

29 "Airbnb Expands Beyond The Home With The Launch Of Trips." 2016. *Airbnb Press Room*. https://press.airbnb.com/airbnb-expands-beyond-the-home-with-the-launch-of-trips/.

30 Concert, AFROHAUS. "AFROHAUS Holiday Concert - Airbnb." Airbnb. https://da.airbnb.com/experiences/107838?location=Kitaa%2C%20Gr%C3%B8nland&source=p2&currentTab=experience_tab&searchId=4a10dfoa-5a20-4b86-9636-613e14b4cb33&recommended_instance_id=389114.

31 Ibid.

32 Ibid.

33 Ibid.

CHAPTER 10

34 Rock Hall. 2018. Your Support Helps Us Tell Rock'S Story. Video. https://www.instagram.com/p/BqsA3yPHnxV/?igshid=xwubrias3998.

35 "About The Rock Hall." Rock & Roll Hall Of Fame. https://www.rockhall.com/visit/about-rock-hall.

36 Sinek, Simon. 2010. How Great Leaders Inspire Action.
    Video. https://www.ted.com/talks/simon_sinek_how_
    great_leaders_inspire_action/up-next.

37 Ibid.

CHAPTER 11

38 Chris, Payne. 2018. "Parahoy! Cruise Day 4 Recap:
    Paramore Gets Personal In Live Q&A, Judah & The Lion
    Talk New Music." Billboard. https://www.billboard.com/
    articles/columns/rock/8301750/paramore-parahoy-
    cruise-2018-day-4-recap.

CHAPTER 12

39 Pareles, Jon, Ben Ratliff, and Jon Caramanica. 2016. "Why
    We'Re Not Making Plans For Coachella And Bonnaroo."
    Nytimes.Com. https://www.nytimes.com/2016/03/19/arts/
    music/summer-music-festivals.html.

40 Ibid.

41 Ibid.

42 Lynch, John. 2018. "Inside Bonnaroo: How The Music
    Festival Doubled Down On Its Roots To Rebound From

Record-Low Attendance In 2016." Business Insider. https://
www.businessinsider.com/bonnaroo-doubled-down-on-
roots-to-rebound-from-record-low-2016-2018-6.

CHAPTER 14

43 Pollard, Alexandra. 2017. "Maggie Rogers On The Song
That Left Pharrell Speechless: 'It Tumbled Out In 15 Minutes.'" *The Guardian.* https://www.theguardian.com/
music/2017/mar/16/maggie-rogers-pharrell-williams-
speechless-tumbled-15-minutes-alaska.

44 "Learn About Zumba Fitness | Zumba Classes." 2019.
Zumba.Com. https://www.zumba.com/en-US/about.

45 Heid, Markham. 2017. "Why Zumba Is Insanely
Good Exercise." *Time.* https://time.com/4696746/
zumba-workout-dance-aerobics/.

CHAPTER 15

46 Forbes. 2014. *Digital Detox At Camp Grounded | Forbes.
Video.* https://www.youtube.com/watch?v=G9IswwrDj2s.

47 Ibid.

48 Atkinson, Katie. 2017. "John Mayer Defies 'Gravity' With Alessia Cara & Brings The Blues To Dive Bar Tour Stop In L.A.: Watch." *Billboard.* https://www.billboard.com/articles/columns/rock/7881881/john-mayer-bud-light-dive-bar-tour-echoplex-los-angeles-concert-recap.

49 Mallenbaum, Carly. 2017. "John Mayer Played One Of is Best Shows Ever At A Dive Bar With Alessia Cara." *USA Today.* https://www.usatoday.com/story/life/entertainthis/2017/07/27/john-mayer-dive-bar-alessia-cara/515406001/.

CHAPTER 19

50 Oxford Dictionaries, s.v. "community," www.oxforddictionaries.com/definition/english/community.

CHAPTER 21

51 "Sustainability." 2019. *Lollapalooza.* https://www.lollapalooza.com/sustainability/.

52 "Bama Works." *Dave Matthews Band.* https://www.davematthewsband.com/bamaworks/

Recipe

Ingredients

_____

_____

_____

_____

_____

_____

_____

_____

_____

_____

_____

_____

_____

_____

_____

_____

_____

Direction

_____

_____

_____

_____

_____

_____

_____

_____

_____

_____

_____

_____

_____

_____

_____

_____

_____

Recipe

Ingredients

_____

_____

_____

_____

_____

_____

_____

_____

_____

_____

_____

_____

_____

_____

Direction

_____

_____

_____

_____

_____

_____

_____

_____

_____

_____

_____

_____

_____

_____

_____

_____

_____

_____

Recipe

Ingredients

_____

_____

_____

_____

_____

_____

_____

_____

_____

_____

_____

_____

_____

_____

_____

Direction

_____

_____

_____

_____

_____

_____

_____

_____

_____

_____

_____

_____

_____

_____

_____

Recipe

Ingredients

Direction

www.ingramcontent.com/pod-product-compliance
Lightning Source LLC
Chambersburg PA
CBHW071521180526
45171CB00002B/334